The book series offers an outlet for cutting-edge research in all areas of political science. Contributions to Political Science (CPS) welcomes theoretically sound and empirically robust monographs, edited volumes and handbooks from a variety of disciplines and approaches on topics such as political theory, comparative politics, democracy, European politics, electoral systems and voting behaviour, public policy and administration, political economy, and related fields.
All titles in this series are peer-reviewed. This book series is indexed in Scopus.

Werner Reutter

Constitutional Courts in the German States

History, Structure, and Functions

Springer

Verfassungs-rechtsprechung," in W. Reutter (ed.), *Verfassungsgerichtsbarkeit in Bundesländern. Theoretische Ansätze, methodische Überlegungen und empirische Befunde* (pp. 203–233). Wiesbaden: Springer VS 2020; "Landesverfassungsgerichte als Verfassungsorgane." In W. Reutter (ed.), *Verfassungsgerichtsbarkeit in Bundesländern. Theoretische Ansätze, methodische Überlegungen und empirische Befunde* (pp. 155–174). Wiesbaden: Springer VS 2020. "Zur Beschlussfähigkeit von Landesverfassungsgerichten. Risiken und Nebenwirkungen des Rechts zur Selbstergänzung," in *ZLVR—Zeitschrift für Landesverfassungsrecht und Landesverwaltungsrecht,* 2/2024, pp. 34–39. I would like to thank Dr. Kitzinger (Kohlhammer Verlag), Dr. Jörn Treibel (Springer VS), Anna Hubbard (European Political Science), Elizabeth Wener (Mohr Siebeck Tübingen), Hannes Berger (ZLVR), Stephan Bröchler, and Benjamin Höhne for providing me with the permission for republication.

The translation of legal terms into a foreign language produces multiple challenges and hurdles. Many German legal terms simply do not exist in American English (e.g., *Popularklage*), while other expressions change their meaning when translated literally. For example, "*Land*" translates as "country," at least literally. However, in this book "*Land*" means "state," i.e., a subnational unit in the Federal Republic. And still other terms have different connotations (such as "*Rechtsstaat*" and "*rule of law*"). I have therefore taken some liberties in transferring German terms into American English. I have also used the terms "judge" and "justice" interchangeably and sometimes stuck to the German expression. I have translated quotations from other sources and put untranslated German terms in italics.

I would like to thank Maria-Lena Muckelbauer and Halyna Tsytskun for their support in gathering data, as well as the state constitutional courts, which willingly provided me with information on the numbers and types of cases received.

Berlin, Germany
June 2024

Werner Reutter

Contents

1 **Introduction: Constitutional Democracy and Constitutional Courts in the German States** ... 1
  1.1 Constitutional Courts in the German States, or What This Book Is About ... 4
  1.2 The Book's Outline and Objectives ... 9
  References ... 12

2 **The Constitutional Court of Berlin: A Case Study** ... 15
  2.1 The Berlin Constitutional Court: Outlining the Subject ... 16
  2.2 The Constitutional Court of the State of Berlin: "A Judicial Body *sui generis*" ... 17
  2.3 Appointment of Justices and Composition of the Constitutional Court of the State of Berlin ... 20
  2.4 The Constitutional Court and Judicialization of Politics in Berlin ... 25
  2.5 The Berlin Constitutional Court as Part of the Political System ... 28
  References ... 30

3 **Democracy, Federalism, and the Rule of Law: Theoretical Perspectives on Constitutional Adjudication in the German States** ... 35
  3.1 State Constitutional Courts and German Constitutional Democracy: Legal Framework ... 36
  3.2 Social Sciences on Constitutional Courts and Constitutional Adjudication: An Overview ... 39
  3.3 Explaining Decision-Making in Constitutional Courts ... 43
  References ... 46

BW	Baden-Württemberg
BW VerfGH	Verfassungsgerichtshof Baden-Württemberg (Constitutional Court of Baden-Württemberg)
BW VerfGHG	Gesetz über den Verfassungsgerichtshof Baden-Württemberg (Act on the Constitutional Court of Baden-Württemberg)
CDU	Christlich Demokratische Union Deutschlands (Christian Democratic Union of Germany)
CSU	Christlich-Soziale Union in Bayern (Christian Social Union in Bavaria)
Drs.	Drucksache (printed matter)
Ed(s).	Editor(s)
et seq.	and the following
EU	European Union
FCC	Federal Constitutional Court
FDP	Freie Demokratische Partei (Free Democratic Party)
FRG	Federal Republic of Germany
GDR	German Democratic Republic (Deutsche Demokratische Republik)
GG	Grundgesetz (Basic Law)
GO	Geschäftsordnung (rules of procedure)
HAM	Hamburg (Hanseatic City)
HES	Hesse
HessStGH	Hessischer Staatsgerichtshof (Hessian State Court of Justice)
HessStGHG	Gesetz über den Staatsgerichtshof Hessen (Law on the State Court of Hesse)
HmbVerf	Verfassung der Freien und Hansestadt Hamburg (Constitution of the Free and Hanseatic City of Hamburg)
HmbVerfG	Hamburgisches Verfassungsgericht (Hamburg Constitutional Court)
KPD	Kommunistische Partei Deutschlands (Communist Party of Germany)
LL/PDS	Linke Liste/Partei des Demokratischen Sozialismus (Left Party/Party of Democratic Socialism)
LP	Legislative period
LS	Lower Saxony
LT	Landtag (state parliament)
LVerfG MW	Landesverfassungsgericht Mecklenburg-Vorpommern (State Constitutional Court of Mecklenburg-Western Pomerania)
LVerfG SAT	Landesverfassungsgericht von Sachsen-Anhalt (State Constitutional Court of Saxony-Anhalt)
LVerfG SH	Schleswig-Holsteinisches Landesverfassungsgericht (Schleswig-Holstein State Constitutional Court)
MP(s)	Member(s) of Parliament
MW	Mecklenburg-Western Pomerania

NdsStGH	Niedersächsischer Staatsgerichtshof (State Court of Justice of Lower Saxony)
No.	Number
NRW	North Rhine-Westphalia
NSDAP	Nationalsozialistische Deutsche Arbeiterpartei (National Socialist German Workers' Party)
NWVBl.	Nordrhein-Westfälische Verwaltungsblätter
para.	Paragraph (Absatz)
PDS	Partei des Demokratischen Sozialismus (Party of Democratic Socialism)
PlPr	Plenarprotokoll (minutes of plenary proceedings)
pp.	pages
RhPfVerf	Verfassung für Rheinland-Pfalz (Constitution for Rhineland-Palatinate)
Rn.	Randnummer (margin number)
RP	Rhineland-Palatinate
SaarlVerfGH	Verfassungsgerichtshof Saarland (Saarland Constitutional Court)
SaarlVerfGHG	Gesetz Nr. 645 über den Verfassungsgerichtshof Saarland (Law No. 645 on the Constitutional Court of Saarland)
SachsAnhVerfGG	Gesetz über das Landesverfassungsgericht Sachsen-Anhalt (Law on the Constitutional Court of Saxony-Anhalt)
SächsVerfGH	Verfassungsgerichtshof des Freistaates Sachsen (Constitutional Court of the Free State of Saxony)
SAT	Saxony-Anhalt
SAY	Saxony (Free State)
SED	Sozialistische Einheitspartei Deutschlands (Socialist Unity Party of Germany)
SH	Schleswig-Holstein
SLD	Saarland
SPD	Sozialdemokratische Partei Deutschlands (Social Democratic Party of Germany)
StPO	Strafprozessordnung (Code of Criminal Procedure)
TH	Thuringia (Free State)
ThürVerfGH	Thüringer Verfassungsgerichtshof (Thuringian Constitutional Court)
ThürVerfGHG	Gesetz über den Thüringer Verfassungsgerichtshof (Act on the Thuringian Constitutional Court)
Verf MV	Verfassung des Landes Mecklenburg-Vorpommern (Constitution of the State of Mecklenburg-Vorpommern)
VerfBW	Verfassung des Landes Baden-Württemberg (Constitution of the State of Baden-Württemberg)
VerfGBbg	Verfassungsgericht des Landes Brandenburg (Constitutional Court of the State of Brandenburg)

List of Tables

Table 1.1 Caseload of State Constitutional Courts (Varying Periods) 8
Table 1.2 State Constitutional Courts: Name and Location (as of March 2020) ... 11
Table 2.1 Constitutional Court Justices in Berlin (as of December 31, 2021) ... 21
Table 2.2 Berlin Constitutional Court: Workload by Type of Proceeding ... 26
Table 3.1 Judicial Decision-Making and Constitutional Courts: Political Science Perspectives (based on B. Rehder) ... 44
Table 4.1 State Constitutions and State Constitutional Courts ... 65
Table 4.2 State Constitutional Courts: First Justices (Without Deputies) ... 69
Table 5.1 State Constitutional Jurisdiction in State Constitutions, in Constitutional Court Laws, and in Rules of Procedure of the State Parliaments ... 75
Table 5.2 State Constitutional Courts: Location, Staff and Budgets (as of May 2016) ... 77
Table 5.3 State Constitutional Courts: Jurisdiction (as of December 2018) ... 81
Table 5.4 State Constitutional Courts: Number of Cases by Type (in Percent and Absolute Numbers; Varying Periods) ... 83
Table 6.1 State Constitutional Justices: Number and Eligibility Criteria ... 91
Table 6.2 Right to Propose Constitutional Justices for Office ... 96
Table 6.3 Elections of Constitutional Justices in Nine States: Number of Candidates and Number of Elected Justices (as of December 31, 2018) ... 97
Table 6.4 Constitutional Justices: Election Processes in State Parliaments ... 100

elections in Fall 2024, or even to take over governmental responsibility, notably the media and some experts (cf. the project on Thuringia on *www.verfassungsblog.de;* Beck et al., 2024) reflect on the role that state constitutional courts could play if an authoritarian populist party comes to power, or is represented in a parliament with such a large majority that it could jeopardize the constitutional bodies' functioning. However, the role and importance of state constitutional courts have been little studied and remain largely unknown. In this book in general, and in this introduction in particular, I will therefore examine and elaborate on the 16 state constitutional courts' contributions to constitutional democracy, and whether they have contributed to the judicialization of politics.

For a long time, political scientists all but ignored constitutional adjudication in the states. This is quite surprising. More than 25 years ago, Konrad Hesse, one of the most influential legal scholars of the Bonn Republic and a justice on the Federal Constitutional Court from 1975 to 1987, provided a chronological diagnosis of constitutional jurisprudence in the Federal Republic of Germany, including the state constitutional courts. "*Verfassungsrechtsprechung im geschichtlichen Wandel* [Constitutional Jurisprudence in Historical Change]" was the title of his essay, in which Hesse (1995) not only attempted to work out the Federal Constitutional Court's contribution to the acceptance and "silent constitutional change" of the Basic Law, but also underlined current problems and future challenges of constitutional jurisdiction in the Federal Republic of Germany (Hesse, 1995, pp. 265ff.). Among the "determining factors" of the supreme constitutional guardian's changing "tasks, position, and scope of action," Hesse named the state constitutional jurisdiction, which had received a "strong boost" from the developments in the then—still—new east German states. State constitutional courts even developed into a real "competitor" of the Federal Constitutional Court. This could also help to reduce the workload of the highest German court, even though the "collision, demarcation, and allocation problems" resulting from this constellation had not been finally clarified (Hesse, 1995, p. 269).

Now, more than a quarter of a century later, one can argue that Hesse was more or less correct in his prediction of the Federal Republic of Germany's subsequent constitutional development and constitutional courts contribution to this process—especially given that the number of cases brought before the Federal Constitutional Court reached a new high of 6811 in 2014. Complaints about the Federal Constitutional Court's (overly) high workload have not been silenced to this day (Bundesverfassungsgericht, 2021, p. 4; Möllers, 2019, pp. 370–372). However, Hesse's reflections also raise the question of the role and significance of state constitutional jurisdiction in the constitutional democracy of the Federal Republic of Germany. Such a broad perspective is justified by the fact that, according to the Federal Constitutional Court's established case law, the Federation and the states must jointly fulfill the "duty to maintain and establish order in accordance with the Basic Law in all parts and levels of the state as a whole" (BVerfGE 56, 298 (322); cf. also BVerfGE 8, 122 (138); BVerfGE 7, 377 (443); BVerfGE 33, 303 (357 et seq.). The duty to "preserve and establish" German constitutional democracy is by no means incumbent on the Federal Constitutional Court alone, but on a "network of constitutional courts." According to the President of the Constitutional Court of Rhineland-Palatinate, Lars Brocker, the state constitutional courts can play an institutionally comparable role for their "state constitution as the Federal Constitutional Court does for the Basic Law" (Brocker, 2021, p. 4). At the same time, the concept of interconnectedness makes it possible to dispense with "simplifying images such as 'equal order, superordination, and subordination'"; instead, researchers should use "aspects of order such as unity, difference and diversity, homogeneity and plurality, demarcation, interplay and interlocking" to capture and qualify the concept of interconnectedness between the courts (Voßkuhle, 2011, p. 11; cf. also Kneip, 2020, p. 25–30).

Following these considerations, I have set myself to working out the importance of state constitutional adjudication in the constitutional court system outlined above and the contributions that state constitutional courts have made to constitutional democracy in Germany in the past, and can make in the future, from a political science perspective. For this purpose, I understand state constitutional courts in the broadest sense as institutions that are to be created and legitimized politically, whose decisions concern the political itself, and which can also have a function in shaping society. This does not change the fact that they are courts *sui generis*, as Gerhard Leibholz had emphasized during the dispute over the Federal Constitutional Court's status in the early 1950s. And he had included state constitutional courts in the Court's memorandum on the status of the Federal Constitutional Court (Statusbericht, 1957; see also Reutter, 2020 and Chap. 5). In addition, the political science approach to constitutional jurisdiction is characterized by a predominantly empirical perspective.

Until a few years ago, however, political scientists ignored state constitutional courts. They considered these constitutional bodies neither in theories of federalism nor in studies of the relationship between constitutional adjudication and democracy (e.g., Scharpf et al., 1976; Lehmbruch, 2000; Laufer & Münch, 2010; Helms et al., 2017). It was only after the turn of the millennium that political scientists found these institutions worthy of closer scrutiny. This interest was fueled by German unification, the establishment of constitutional courts in the eastern German states (including Berlin) and Schleswig-Holstein, and the increasing relevance of state politics (Reutter, 2022, pp. 11f.; Gundling & Güpner, 2021). Such changes prompted political scientists to conduct first studies addressing the role of state constitutional courts and to shed light on their contribution to constitutional development in the states and the Federal Republic of Germany (Flick, 2011; Reutter, 2022, pp. 7–14).

This delayed engagement with the "supreme guardians" of the state constitutions may have contributed to the fact that the view long prevalent in legal scholarship (and still held by some) that state constitutional courts have neither the institutional resources nor the competences to shape the states' constitutional lives has found no corresponding echo in current political science studies (Freund, 1994; Leisner, 1972; Bachof, 1968; Gärditz, 2013). Martina Flick (2008, p. 253) even diagnoses

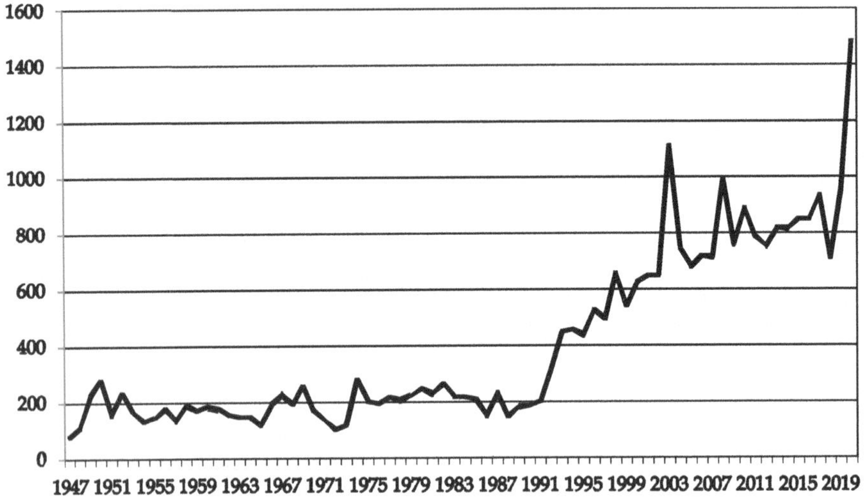

Source: self-conducted survey; information from the state constitutional courts; as of Dec. 31st, 2020.

Fig. 1.1 Workload of State Constitutional Courts: Registered Cases (Cumulative; 1947–2020; as of Dec. 31st, 2020)

court), to 832 per year (2010 to 2020; 56 per year and court). In 2020, the number of new cases filed peaked at almost 1500.

There are institutional, jurisdictional, and event-related reasons for these changes: On the institutional side, the number of state constitutional courts has steadily increased. The three courts established before the Basic Law in Bavaria (1947), Hesse (1948). and Rhineland-Palatinate (1947) were followed by six state constitutional courts established after the Basic Law came into effect in Bremen (1949), Baden-Württemberg (1955), North Rhine-Westphalia (1952), Hamburg (1953), Lower Saxony (1957), and Saarland (1959) as well as seven state constitutional courts established after unification in Berlin (1992), Brandenburg (1993), Mecklenburg-Western Pomerania (1995), Saxony (1993), Saxony-Anhalt (1993), Thuringia (1995), and Schleswig-Holstein (2008). Berlin and Schleswig-Holstein proved the exceptions. Although the constitution of (West) Berlin, which entered into force in 1950, provided for a constitutional court in Art. 72 (1), the law necessary to put the constitutional stipulation into practice was never passed. The article was finally suspended in 1974 (Reutter, 2017; Pestalozza, 1983). Until the two German states' unification, the city thus remained a "blank spot on the map of German constitutional adjudication" (Finkelnburg, 2001, p. 15; Pestalozza, 1983), because its special Allied status, valid until 1990, prevented its residents and other persons entitled to file applications from going to Karlsruhe and from appealing to their own state constitutional court (Chap. 2).

Schleswig-Holstein, which has had its own state constitutional court since 2008, was a different case (Flick Witzig, 2017). In Art. 37 of its provisional state constitution of 1949 *(Landessatzung)* and Art. 44 of its constitution of 1990, Schleswig-Holstein had transferred the competence to resolve political disputes between state organs to the Federal Constitutional Court by way of a so-called "borrowed administration" (*Organleihe*). In other words, the Second Senate of the Federal Constitutional Court acted as Schleswig-Holstein's state constitutional court until 2008 and had to make decisions in 26 proceedings concerning issues limited to this state (Bundesverfassungsgericht, 2021, p. 6).

Notwithstanding these exceptions, it should be noted that since 2008, there has been a dual structure of constitutional adjudication in Germany encompassing the federal territory in total. Germany holds a comprehensive network of federal and state constitutional courts (Voßkuhle, 2011; Brocker, 2021), one supplemented and completed by European courts that I will, however, disregard in the following, as EU law has not yet gained relevance as a subject matter or as a standard for state constitutional adjudication (Lindner, 2020).

At the same time and on the jurisdictional side, the procedural law has been successively rounded off. Formally, the states' constitutional jurisdiction comprises a total of 17 types of proceedings. A single court can have between 6 and 11 such types (Reutter, 2022, p. 75). Quite a few of these provided for by law have rarely or never been used (e.g., impeachment of ministers or members of parliament). Nevertheless, the jurisdictional catalogues of the state constitutional courts in Rhineland-Palatinate, Baden-Württemberg, North Rhine-Westphalia, and Lower Saxony have been expanded. Individual constitutional complaints can be lodged with the first three constitutional courts since 1992, 2013, and 2019 respectively; since 1993, local authorities can lodge complaints with the Lower Saxony State Court of Justice if they believe that their right to local self-government has been violated. This consolidation has increased caseloads in all four courts. After the introduction of the constitutional complaint, the number of cases filed with the Constitutional Court of Rhineland-Palatinate rose from an average of 7 per year (until 1992) to about 33 (since 1993). The Constitutional Court of Baden-Württemberg experienced a similar increase in the number of cases filed, from 11.8 per year to 34.4 (since 1993). Ultimately, the increase in the number of cases was due to specific events and was therefore "exogenously induced" (Lembcke & Güpner, 2018, p. 104). This is because the short-term boom in applications was a response to municipal territorial reforms or Corona-related measures (2019/20).

example to illustrate how a state constitutional court functions and what role it can play in a state's political order. In the third chapter, I adopt a more abstract stance on the subject, dealing with the constitutional foundations of state constitutional adjudication in general. I also present and discuss theories of judicial decision-making.

In the fourth chapter, I look at how constitutional courts came to exist. In principle, many legal scholars and political scientists see constitutional adjudication as a reaction to totalitarian or authoritarian regimes. Logically, many newly established democracies set up such institutions to protect the constitution and act as its guardians (Steinsdorff, 2010; Möllers, 2019). In this chapter, I will examine whether similar motives can be found in the German states and how this anti-totalitarian impulse was implemented in the establishment of state constitutional courts. I will also tackle whether and to what extent the establishment of state constitutional courts marks a new beginning similar to that of the Federal Constitutional Court.

In the fifth chapter, I describe and analyze the institutional requirements of state constitutional adjudication. I examine these constitutional bodies' place in the political systems of the states, as well as their structures and mode of operation. I then devote the sixth chapter to the personal dimension of state constitutional jurisdiction. In it, I describe the different election and appointment procedures, the composition of these courts as a resource for the administration of justice, and the question of how a justice's term of office comes to an end. In doing so, I am addressing whether and in what form constitutional courts can be protected against the constitution's enemies, a question that has become particularly controversial as some state parliaments have elected candidates proposed by the right-wing extremist AfD *(Alternative für Deutschland)* as justices to the respective state constitutional court.

In the seventh chapter, I focus on the state constitutional courts' rulings. This includes, on the one hand, analyzing their workload profiles (number and type of proceedings over time, in comparison to, and by type of, proceedings) and, on the other hand, attempting to find causal factors for constitutional court decisions. In the concluding eighth chapter, I return to the question of whether and how state constitutional courts can contribute to what has been coined "militant" or "defensive democracy" *(wehrhafte Demokratie)*.

Some preliminary remarks are needed regarding this book's subject. Many researchers usually present the states' structures, institutions, and policies in a conceptually generalized form—as *the* state parliaments, *the* state parties, *the* states, or *the* state constitutional courts. I use such generalizing terminology as well, under the assumption that similarities can be densified in such a way that the subject's essence can be captured by a single term. In this respect, there is good reason to speak of state constitutional adjudication or state constitutional courts. For they all share so many and such vital characteristics that the use of one single ideal-typical term that includes all 16 institutions not only makes sense but promotes knowledge.

However, there are differences as well as similarities among state constitutional courts (Table 1.2). And these differences are not only empirically interesting but have theoretical implications as well. Differences can be empirically revealing because they (may) lead to conclusions about the importance and functioning of a state's constitutional court. Theoretically, such findings are significant because diversity is a structural and functional element of any federal system. Federalism

Table 1.2 State Constitutional Courts: Name and Location (as of March 2020)

State	Name (abbreviation)	Location (year of establishment)
BW	Constitutional Court of Baden-Württemberg (BW VerfGH)	Stuttgart (1955)
BAV	Bavarian Constitutional Court (BayVerfGH)	Munich (1947)
BER	Constitutional Court of the State of Berlin (BerlVerfGH)	Berlin (1992)
BB	Constitutional Court of the State of Brandenburg (VerfGBbg)	Potsdam (1993)
BRE	State Court of Justice of the Free Hanseatic City of Bremen (BremStGH)	Bremen (1949)
HAM	Hamburg Constitutional Court (HmbVerfG)	Hamburg (1953)
HES	Hessian State Court of Justice (HessStGH)	Wiesbaden (1948)
MW	State Constitutional Court of Mecklenburg-Western Pomerania (LVerfG MW)	Greifswald (1995)
LS	Lower Saxony State Court of Justice (NdsStGH)	Bückeburg (1957)
NRW	Constitutional Court for the State of North Rhine-Westphalia (VerfGH NRW)	Münster (1952)
RP	Constitutional Court of Rhineland-Palatinate (VerfGH Rh.-Pf.)	Koblenz (1949)
SLD	Saarland Constitutional Court (SaarlVerfGH)	Saarbrücken (1959)
SAY	Constitutional Court of the Free State of Saxony (SächsVerfGH)	Leipzig (1993)
SAT	State Constitutional Court of Saxony-Anhalt (LVerfG SAT)	Dessau-Roßlau (1993)
SH	Schleswig-Holstein State Constitutional Court (LVerfG SH)	Schleswig (2008)
TH	Thuringian Constitutional Court (ThürVerfGH)	Weimar (1995)

Source: Self-compilation

presupposes divergences between the states and allows—even demands—differences between the constitutional bodies. This also applies to the constitutional courts of the states. The relevance of these considerations can be illustrated by comparing some features of the existing constitutional courts. For example, state constitutional courts were established in different historical periods. They also vary in terms of location, number of justices, and caseload. There existed four constitutional courts before the adoption of the Basic Law,[1] five were added in the 1950s, six after reunification in 1990, and one after the turn of the millennium. It goes without saying that the different historical and legal frameworks did not remain without consequences for the respective constitutional courts' designs. Whether a constitutional court was established before the Basic Law came into effect, immediately afterwards, or following the successful revolution in the GDR made a difference.

Furthermore, in eight states the constitutional court is located in the state capital, and in as many it is located in other cities of the respective state. The choice of location was by no means intended to make possible "proximity to politics", as Lorenz (2017, p. 105) assumes for the case of Brandenburg. Rather, the decision to locate

[1] In addition, there were the state courts of Justice of Baden, Württemberg-Hohenzollern, and Württemberg-Baden, which were established in 1947/48 and dissolved when the three states merged to form Baden-Württemberg in 1952.

Lembcke, O. W. (2017). Thüringer Verfassungsgerichtshof. In W. Reutter (Ed.), *Landesverfassungsgerichte. Entwicklung—Aufbau—Funktionen* (pp. 389–420). Springer VS.

Lembcke, O. W., & Güpner, M. (2018). Analyse der Landesverfassungsgerichtsbarkeit in vergleichender Absicht. Ein Beitrag zur Typologisierung und Quantifizierung. *Zeitschrift für Landesverfassungsrecht und Landesverwaltungsrecht (ZLVR), 3*(3), 94–104. https://www.zlvr.de/archiv/

Lindner, J. F. (2020). Landesverfassungsgerichte und europäische Integration. In W. Reutter (Ed.), *Verfassungsgerichtsbarkeit in Bundesländern. Theoretische Perspektiven, methodische Überlegungen und empirische Befunde* (pp. 385–400). Springer VS.

Lorenz, A. (2017). Das Verfassungsgericht Brandenburg als politisiertes Organ? Möglichkeiten und Grenzen politischer Einflussnahme. In W. Reutter (Ed.), *Landesverfassungsgerichte. Entwicklung—Aufbau—Funktionen* (pp. 105–128). Springer VS.

LVerfGE. (1993ff.). *Entscheidungen der Verfassungsgerichte der Länder.* Hrsgg. von den Mitgliedern der Gerichte. de Gruyter.

Möllers, C. (2019). Legalität, Legitimität und Legitimation des Bundesverfassungsgerichts. In M. Jestaedt, O. Lepsius, C. Möllers, & C. Schönberger (Eds.), *Das entgrenzte Gericht. Eine kritische Bilanz nach sechzig Jahren Bundesverfassungsgericht* (pp. 281–422, 3rd ed.). suhrkamp.

Papier, H.-J. (2002). Die Bedeutung der Landesverfassungsgerichtsbarkeit im Verhältnis zur Bundesverfassungsgerichtsbarkeit. In H. Sodan (Ed.), *Zehn Jahre Berliner Verfassungsgerichtsbarkeit. Ansprachen anläßlich des Festaktes am 24. Mai 2002* (pp. 19–34). Carl Heymanns Verlag.

Papier, H.-J. (2020). Verfassungsgerichtsrechtsprechung und ihre Wirkung auf föderale Einheiten. In Europäisches Zentrum für Föderalismus-Forschung (Ed.), *Jahrbuch des Föderalismus 2020. Föderalismus, Subsidiarität und Regionen in Europa* (pp. 25–33). Nomos.

Pestalozza, C. (1983). Berlin ohne Verfassungsgericht. In C. Starck & K. Stern (Eds.), *Landesverfassungsgerichtsbarkeit. Teilband I. Geschichte, Organisation, Rechtsvergleichung* (pp. 183–230). Nomos.

Reutter, W. (2017). Der Verfassungsgerichtshof des Landes Berlin. In W. Reutter (Ed.), *Landesverfassungsgerichte in der Bundesrepublik Deutschland. Entwicklung—Aufbau—Funktionen* (pp. 77–104). Springer VS.

Reutter, W. (2020). Zum Status der Landesverfassungsgerichte als Verfassungsorgane. In W. Reutter (Ed.), *Verfassungsgerichtsbarkeit in Bundesländern. Theoretische Perspektiven, methodische Überlegungen und empirische Befunde* (pp. 155–174). Springer VS.

Reutter, W. (2022). *Landesverfassungsgerichtsbarkeit.* Verlag W. Kohlhammer.

Scharpf, F. W., Reissert, B., & Schnabel, F. (1976). *Politikverflechtung. Theorie und Empirie des kooperativen Föderalismus in der Bundesrepublik.* Scriptor.

Sommer, C. (2017). Das sachsen-anhaltische Landesverfassungsgericht: "Hüter der Verfassung". In H. Träger & S. Priebus (Eds.), *Politik und Regieren in Sachsen-Anhalt* (pp. 89–102). Springer VS.

Statusbericht. (1957). Der Status des Bundesverfassungsgerichts. Material—Gutachten, Denkschriften und Stellungnahmen mit einer Einleitung von Gerhard Leibholz. *Jahrbuch des öffentlichen Rechts der Gegenwart (N.F.), 6*, 109–221.

Steinsdorff, S. v. (2010). Verfassungsgerichte als Demokratie-Versicherung? Ursachen und Grenzen der wachsenden Bedeutung juristischer Politikkontrolle. In K. H. Schrenk & M. Soldner (Eds.), *Analyse demokratischer Regierungssysteme* (pp. 479–498). Springer VS.

Voßkuhle, A. (2011). Die Landesverfassungsgerichtsbarkeit im föderalen und europäischen Verfassungsgerichtsverbund. *Jahrbuch des öffentlichen Rechts der Gegenwart* (N.F.), *59*, 215–243.

Weigl, M. (2017). Der Bayerische Verfassungsgerichtshof. In W. Reutter (Ed.), *Landesverfassungsgerichte. Entwicklung—Aufbau—Funktionen* (pp. 53–76). Springer VS.

Zuck, R. (1997). Die Entlastung des Bundesverfassungsgerichts: Fragen zur Benda—Kommission. *Zeitschrift für Rechtspolitik, 30*(3), 95–99. Retrieved from https://www.jstor.org/stable/23424672

Chapter 2
The Constitutional Court of Berlin: A Case Study

The power and influence of a state constitutional court varies from state to state (Reutter 2022b). A case study of the Constitutional Court of the State of Berlin will therefore illustrate how and on what basis such a court functions, what influence it can muster, and what contribution it might make to the political order. The Constitutional Court of the State of Berlin is one with a broad jurisdictional profile. It is frequently called upon. It receives significantly more cases each year than most other state constitutional courts, and even more than the Federal Constitutional Court in terms of population. Nevertheless, in many respects it is a typical court—for one, it has made decisions in important areas that are of significance to state policy. This court is therefore particularly suited to illustrating the different functions state constitutional courts perform. At the same time, this chapter provides an in-depth view of this type of constitutional body, its composition, and its possible power.

The data on the Berlin Constitutional Court used in this chapter can be found at https://www.sowi.hu-berlin.de/de/forschung/projekte/LVerfGe and was retrieved from parliamentary documentation of the House of Representatives (https://pardok.parlament-berlin.de/portala/start.tt.html) and the Constitutional Court's website (https://www.berlin.de/gerichte/sonstige-gerichte/verfassungsgerichtshof/). In addition, Simone Köhler (Constitutional Court of Berlin) provided me with information on the number and type of submissions, as she has done on several occasions. My special thanks go to her. The Constitutional Court's decision can be found at http://www.gerichtsentscheidungen.berlin-brandenburg.de/ and http://www.juris.de/jportal/nav/startseite/startseite.jsp. In addition, the annual collection of decisions published jointly by 13 state constitutional courts contains a number of important decisions and judgments; it is cited as: LVerfGE 1993ff. Which decisions are published there is determined by the plenum.

W. Reutter, *Constitutional Courts in the German States*, Contributions to Political Science, https://doi.org/10.1007/978-3-031-64751-2_2

called for a nine-member constitutional court. These members would have been elected by a three-quarters majority of the Berlin parliament, with four of those selected being professional judges. In such a constellation, minority groups holding a quarter of parliamentary seats would have had a decisive influence. In addition, non-lawyers—so-called *Laienrichter*, or lay judges with no legal degree—could have dominated the court (Wille, 1993, p. 29). But the election of the constitutional justices scheduled for February 21st, 1991, failed, primarily because of the planned compensation scheme, which was so extraordinarily generous that it encountered resistance even from the judges to be appointed (Wille, 1993, p. 30). As a result, the Grand Coalition that had been in office since January 1991 amended both the law on the Constitutional Court as well as Art. 72 of the (then in force) Berlin Constitution.

Like all Berlin constitutional bodies, the Berlin Constitutional Court has been based on a hierarchically tiered legal structure since its foundation (Pfennig & Neumann, 2000).[2] Since 1995, it has been based on Art. 84 of the Berlin Constitution (*Verfassung von Berlin*, VvB), which provides the court with an institutional guarantee and contains regulations on the election of justices as well as the court's composition and jurisdiction. With the Act on the Constitutional Court (BerlVerfGHG), this basic norm was made more specific with regard to the status, election procedure, composition, organization, and procedural regulations (Bahl, 1993). Finally, the Constitutional Court regulates its internal affairs with its own rules of procedure. According to the Berlin state constitution, the Court is part of the administration of justice (*Rechtspflege*). Nevertheless, its status as a constitutional body (*Verfassungsorgan*) is undisputed: It is "autonomous" and "independent" (§ 1 (1) BerlVerfGHG). Like the Federal Constitutional Court and the other state constitutional courts, the Berlin Constitutional Court is a "judicial body *sui generis*" (Statusbericht, 1957, p. 120) because it decides on political matters in legal form. It is both a constitutional body and a court. This includes the fact that it makes its decisions free from instructions, draws up and manages its budget independently, and regulates its internal affairs autonomously (Starck, 1983, p. 165 f.; Reutter, 2020c; Chap. 5).

In Berlin, citizens can access the Constitutional Court almost free of charge. The Berlin budget for 2021 foresees about 0.8 million euros for this court. In 2020, the city-state thus ranked third in terms of spending on these constitutional bodies (Reutter, 2022a, p. 79). In the 2021 budget, this item accounted for just 0.02 per thousand (!) and cost each resident just 21 cents per year. In real terms, the Constitutional Court's budget doubled from about 250,000 Euro (1993) to 528,505 Euro (2021; base year 2015; in nominal terms, it tripled to 802,000 Euro (2021)).

history of the Berlin Constitutional Court, see Pestalozza, 1991; Sodan, 2002, 2010; Wille, 1993; Heimann, 2001; Wilke, 1991; Reutter, 2017, p. 78–81.

[2] Constitution of Berlin (VvB) of November 23rd, 1995 (GVBl. p. 779), last amended by the Act of May 17th, 2021 (GVBl, p. 502); Act on the Constitutional Court (BerlVerfGHG) of November 8th, 1990, last amended by the Act of January 22nd, 2021 (GVBl. p. 75); Rules of Procedure of the Constitutional Court of the State of Berlin (BerlVerfGHGO) of December 6th, 1994, completely revised on January 22nd, 2016 (GVBl. No. 5, p. 53 et seq.)

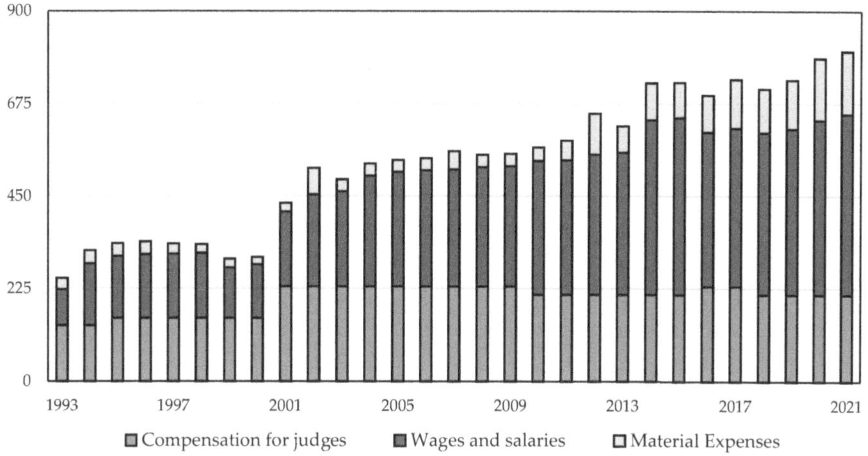

Source: Senatsverwaltung für Finanzen 1993ff.; Einzelplan 02.

Fig. 2.1 Budgets for the Constitutional Court of Berlin (1993 to 2021; in Nominal Prices, in Thousands of Euros)

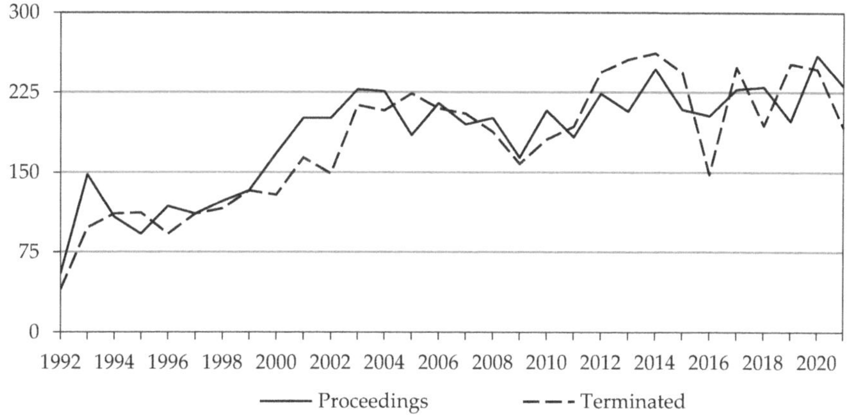

a) In 2007, an additional 76 cases were declared "settled"; from 2012, decisions on the issuance of an interim injunction were counted separately in constitutional complaints.

Source: Verfassungserichtshof 2022, as of December 31st, 2021)

Fig. 2.2 Constitutional Court of Berlin: Cases Submitted and Terminated (1992–2021)

The increases are mainly due to the rising number of cases and the thus larger staff (Figs. 2.1 and 2.2; Senatsverwaltung für Finanzen 1993ff.).[3]

[3]According to § 13 VerfGHG, justices receive a monthly basic allowance of 276 €; presidents 399 €, vice presidents 337 €. In addition, there is a case-related expense allowance of 61 € for decisions and 245 € for decisions on the merits (rapporteurs receive double this amount). For constitutional court judges who are civil servants, the basic compensation is halved (as of 2022).

As in other states, Berlin's constitutional justices are elected "by secret ballot" and "without debate," requiring two-thirds of the votes cast (Reutter, 2018, 2020b). The president of the House of Representatives is responsible for appointing and swearing in justices. As a rule, it fell to the governing mayor or his Senate Chancellery to request that the House of Representatives hold elections (AH Drs. 13/3209, 13/3601, 14/184, Drs. 15/2495; Drs. 18/3746). The President of the House of Representatives or the Senator for Justice also informed the Berlin Parliament which justices were retiring and when, and whether professional, male, and/or female justices were to be elected. However, according to Art. 40 (2) of the Berlin Constitution, only the parliamentary parties have a legal right of nomination. Under these conditions, the Berlin House of Representatives filled 41 positions at the Constitutional Court in a total of 12 elections until the end of 2021 (including the election of Margret Diwell as the court's president in 2007). Three of the candidates proposed by the PDS and the Left Party did not receive the necessary majority of votes.

According to Sascha Kneip (2020, pp. 36–38), a constitutional court can decide independently and have an integrating effect if its justices enjoy broad support and minority groups have a say in election procedures (see also Reutter, 2022a, pp. 87–105; 2020b, p. 210; 2021a; Chap. 6). This requires a "supermajority." In addition, the Constitutional Court must include some candidates proposed and supported by the minority groups themselves. Measured by these criteria, the Berlin Constitutional Court must be considered independent and integrative, not only legally but also politically. At the very least, its composition faithfully reflects the weight of the parties represented in the regional parliament, the House of Representatives (*Abgeordnetenhaus*). Even the Pirate Party *(Piratenpartei)* was granted a seat on the Constitutional Court, despite its short parliamentary existence. Only the Left Party appears to be "underrepresented" in the Constitutional Court, as it provided 15.8% of all MPs between 1990 and 2021, but nominated only 9.8% of the constitutional justices (Fig. 2.3).

Sascha Kneip (2020) argues that the manner in which constitutional justices were being elected help to keep a Court independent. In Berlin, almost all political groups usually supported the elected constitutional justices. For example, the average proportion of "yes" votes in such elections (80.7% of all members of parliament) is far higher than the majority on which the Berlin governments have been able to rely in the Berlin state parliament since 1990 (61.8%). In the 16th legislative period (2006–2011), the calculated difference was as high as 38.4% (Fig. 2.4). Only in the 12th legislative period (1990–1994) did the members of the ruling parties CDU and SPD not unanimously vote for the proposed candidates. Moreover, elected justices can claim far more votes than legally required. This is because, on average, the proportion of "yes" votes among all votes cast was almost 20 percentage points above the two-thirds majority required by Art. 84 (1) VvB (see also Reutter, 2018).

In Berlin, the justices of the constitutional court are elected for a single seven-year term of office. Although this is intended to allow for long-term planning of judicial appointments, the majority of constitutional justices have had to remain in office on an acting basis after their seven-year terms expired. On average, Berlin Constitutional

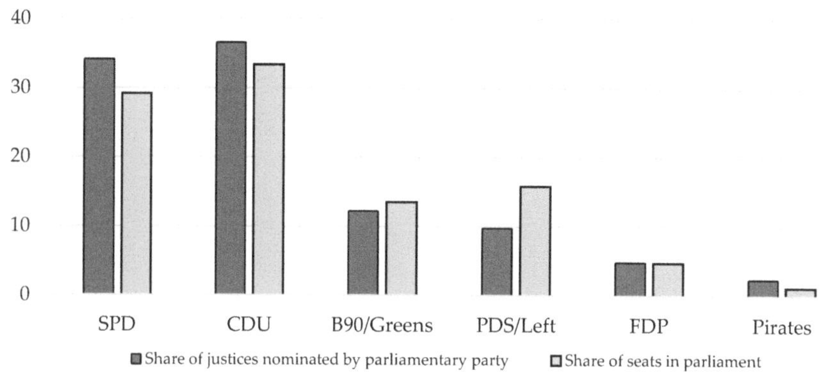

a) Including Margret Diwell's election as President of the Constitutional Court; share of justices nominated by the respective parliamentary party and elected by the House of Representatives in relation to all elected justices; share of seats held by the parliamentary party in the House of Representatives; average values; beginning of the legislative periods.

Source: self-conducted survey, Parlamentsdokumentation, Reutter 2018, p. 491.

Fig. 2.3 Berlin Constitutional Court: Composition by Proposing Parliamentary Party (in Percent; 1992–2021)

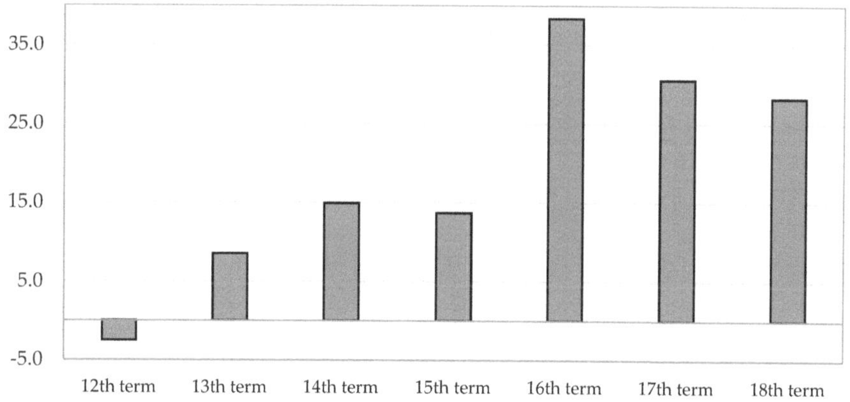

a) The figure shows the difference between the ruling parties' shares of seats (at the beginning of each legislative term) and the share of votes that constitutional court justices received at their respective election (in each case as a percentage of all MPs). It includes Margret Diwell's election as President of the Constitutional Court. For the 14th term (1999/2001), the SPD and the Green party had a minority government starting on June 16, 2001.

Sources: self-conducted survey, Abgeordnetenhaus PlPr 12/27, p. 2304 and 2314; 12/87, p. 7520; 13/29, p. 2240; 13/54, p. 3973f.; 14/6, p. 229f.; 15/52, p. 4360f.; 16/10, p. 796; 16/14, p. 114; 17/10, p. 715; 17/51, p. 5261; 18/48, p. 5725; 18/55, p. 6650; Parlamentsdokumentation des Abgeordnetenhauses Berlin; Reutter 2018, p. 491)

Fig. 2.4 Elections of Constitutional Justices: Majorities (as a Percentage of all Members of Parliament; 1992 to 2021)

cases registered between 1992 and 2021 (Table 2.2). However, only 3–4% of the constitutional complaints successfully achieved their desired result. Of the 174 complaints evaluated using the above index, two—both referendums—had "strength" ratings above 4.5. This type of procedure therefore has an inclusive effect, as it allows "any person" access to the Constitutional Court, but it is almost never associated with judicialization effects. Although constitutional complaints can be used in Berlin to control state action retroactively, they are not a means of shaping the political will prospectively.

Disputes between state organs are genuinely "political proceedings." They are adversarial in nature, the plaintiff and defendant are constitutional bodies (or parts thereof), and the disputes decided in such proceedings are truly political in nature. The highest constitutional bodies or parties "which are vested with their own rights by the Constitution of Berlin or by the rules of procedure of the House of Representatives" (§ 14 No. 1 BerlVerfGHG) are entitled to file a case. By the end of 2021, the Constitutional Court had received 106 such legal actions. It is true that the

Table 2.2 Berlin Constitutional Court: Workload by Type of Proceeding[a]

	1992–2001	2002–2011	2012–2021	1992–2021
Total constitutional complaints	1137	1946	2127	5210
– Penal system/criminal proceedings	332	460	460	1252
– Rent/lease etc.[b]	153	259	219	631
– Press law	3	11	2	16
– Property right[c]	16	60	3	79
– Other civil matters[d]	260	568	750	1578
– Financial social and labor law proceedings	76	180	238	494
– Other administrative disputes	159	248	217	624
– Deportation, residence, asylum, etc.	100	51	47	198
– Constitutional complaint §51 (2) VerfGHG	24	62	34	120
– Corona Ordinance	0	0	81	81
– Other constitutional complaints[e]	14	47	76	137
Judicial reviews (abstract/concrete)	4	5	6	15
Disputes between state organs	31	27	48	106
Electoral law/election audit	33	12	49	94
Popular initiatives etc. (§14 (7) VerfGHG)	2	5	5	12
Other procedures	50	11	2	63
Total workload[f]	1257	2006	2237	5500

[a] Including cassation, resistance, revocation of driving license, private prosecution
[b] Including land restitution, residential property
[c] Including family law and FGG matters
[d] Including investment decisions (1993: 1), formation of district offices (1992: 5, 1993: 1, 1995: 2), reorganization treaty (1996: 5); Lawyers' Court (2015: 1), compensation law (2015: 1)
[e] Including objection procedures for referendums
[f] The sum total of incoming cases by type of procedure differs slightly in some cases from the figures provided by the Constitutional Court
Sources: Reutter, 2017, p. 94f.; Körting & Schmidt, 1998, p. 125; Verfassungsgerichtshof 2022

resulting decisions protected or specified the information and participation rights of the parliament and of individual members of parliamentarians.[5] However, only one of the 30 decisions evaluated with the above-mentioned index had lasting consequences for the legislature (the exception was the temporary injunction of July 29, 1993; BerlVerfGH Az. 65 A/93). In such proceedings, the Constitutional Court acts exclusively as a body for conflict resolution. It allows disputes about the political order to be transferred to non-political legal proceedings. In this way, the system's functioning is ensured.

Proceedings to review passed laws are considered the core of constitutional adjudication (see also Flick 2009). However, such proceedings—be they concrete or abstract—are rare in Berlin. On average, a justice elected to serve for 7 years has to decide only once every 2 years whether a law or legal norm conforms to the Constitution. In total, judicial review proceedings account for only 0.3% of all proceedings (15 out of 5500). Specialized courts (§ 46 (1) of the Constitutional Court Law) submit a norm to the Constitutional Court for review just as seldom as the Senate or members of the House of Representatives question the constitutionality of a law (§ 43 of the Constitutional Court Law). Even if individual decisions have had far-reaching consequences—such as the privatization of water utilities (BerlVerfGH 42/99) or the budget of the state of Berlin for the years 2002–2003 (BerlVerfGH 125/02)—it is difficult to see how such a procedure could have changed the decision-making structure of Berlin's governmental system. The Berlin Constitutional Court has not prejudged the content of decisions made by the state legislature but has at best corrected them retrospectively (see also Grimm, 2021, p. 50).

Review of elections: Since 1992, the Berlin Constitutional Court has recorded 94 proceedings for the review of elections, 39 of which concerned the 2021 elections alone. The court is called upon to review the validity of Berlin elections and possible seat losses on the basis of such complaints, which can be filed by voters, candidates, the State Election Commissioner, parliamentary groups, parties, and other players involved in elections (§ 40 (3) nos. 1 to 3 BerlVerfGHG). The Constitutional Court has also issued a number of important decisions in this area, some of which have had far-reaching consequences (see BerlVerfGH 155/11; BerlVerfGH 137A/01, 137/01, 139A01, 139/01, 142A/01, 142/A, BerlVerfGH 169/06 and 154/21). Overall, however, only one of the 14 decisions analyzed can be classified as mid-strength. In this case as well, the Constitutional Court for the most part acted in an ex-post-controlling manner. This also applies to its November 16th, 2022, decision on the September 2021 elections to the House of Representatives (BerlVerfGH 154/21), which I did not include in the analysis. The decision had far-reaching consequences. However, the Constitutional Court acts as a supervisory body in such

[5] For example, the court strengthened the right of MPs to inspect files and financial planning (VerfGH 57/98, 217/04; 159/10, 92/14; 217/04; 31/15), sanctioned restrictions on non-attached MPs' rights of participation as constitutional (VerfGH 67/12), and declared the premature dissolution of the House of Representatives in 2001 to be lawful (VerfGH 137 A/01, 137/01, 139 A/01, 139/01, 142).

References

Abgeordnetenhaus Berlin. (1990ff.). *Plenarprotokolle und Drucksachen. Parlamentsdokumentation des Abgeordnetenhauses Berlin.* Retrieved from http://pardok.parlament-berlin.de

Bahl, J. (1993). Zum Gesetz über den Berliner Verfassungsgerichtshof. *Neue Zeitschrift für Verwaltungsrecht, 44*(1), 44–47.

Brocker, L. (2021). Landesverfassungsgerichtsbarkeit(en). Von Verbundstrategien und Gravitationsfeldern. *Die öffentliche Verwaltung, 74*(1), 1–11.

Diwell, M. (2008). Begrüßung. In M. Diwell (Ed.), *Chancen, Möglichkeiten und Risiken der Rechtsprechung. Verfassungsgerichtshof des Landes Berlin. Ansprachen anlässlich des Festaktes am 29. November 2007* (pp. 1–8). Carl Heymanns Verlag.

Diwell, M. (2012). Geburtstagswünsche. In S. Schudoma (Ed.), *Zwanzig Jahre Berliner Verfassungsgerichtsbarkeit. Ansprachen anlässlich des Festaktes am 19. Juni 2012* (pp. 29–34). Carl Heymanns Verlag.

Finkelnburg, K. (2001). Die ersten acht Jahre des Verfassungsgerichtshofes des Landes Berlin. In Präsident des Verfassungsgerichtshofes des Landes Berlin (Ed.), *Wechsel und Kontinuität im Verfassungsgerichtshof des Landes Berlin. Ansprachen anläßlich des Festaktes am 14. April 2000* (pp. 13–20). Carl Heymanns Verlag.

Flick, M. (2009). Oppositionelle Akteure als Kläger vor den Landesverfassungsgerichten. *Zeitschrift für Vergleichende Politikwissenschaft, 3*(2), 283–302.

Flick, M. (2011). *Organstreitverfahren vor den Landesverfassungsgerichten: Eine politikwissenschaftliche Untersuchung*. Peter Lang.

Freund, L. (1994). 40 Jahre Staatsgerichtshof Baden-Württemberg. *Baden-Württembergische Verwaltungspraxis, 21*(1), 1–3.

Führer, R. (2001). Der Verfassungsgerichtshof des Landes Berlin als Hüter der Verfassung. In Präsident des Verfassungsgerichtshofes des Landes Berlin (Ed.), *Wechsel und Kontinuität im Verfassungsgerichtshof des Landes Berlin. Ansprachen anläßlich des Festaktes am 14. April 2000* (pp. 9–12). Carl Heymanns Verlag.

Grimm, D. (2021). *Verfassungsgerichtsbarkeit*. Suhrkamp.

Grunert, B. (2000). Mit der Wahl ging ein ewiger Parteienstreit zu Ende. *Der Tagesspiegel*, March 9, 2000. Retrieved from http://www.tagesspiegel.de/berlin/mit-der-wahl-ging-ein-ewiger-parteienstreit-zu-ende/128422.html

Heimann, H. M. (2001). *Die Entstehung der Verfassungsgerichtsbarkeit in den neuen Ländern und in Berlin*. Verlag Franz Vahlen.

Hund, M. (2012). Würdigung der ausgeschiedenen Präsidentin und Richter. Einführung der neuen Präsidentin und Richter. In S. Schudoma (Ed.), *Zwanzig Jahre Berliner Verfassungsgerichtsbarkeit. Ansprachen anlässlich des Festaktes am 19. Juni 2012* (pp. 21–28). Carl Heymanns Verlag.

Hund, M. (2014). Rückblick. In S. Schudoma (Ed.), *Zwanzig Jahre Berliner Verfassungsgerichtsbarkeit. Ansprachen anlässlich des Festaktes am 19. Juni 2012* (pp. 29–62). Carl Heymanns Verlag.

Kneip, S. (2020). Verfassungsgerichte und Demokratie in Bund und Ländern. In W. Reutter (Ed.), *Verfassungsgerichtsbarkeit in Bundesländern. Theoretische Perspektiven, methodische Überlegungen und empirische Befunde* (pp. 25–48). Springer VS.

Körting, E., & Schmidt, D. (1998). Der Verfassungsgerichtshof des Landes Berlin. *Landes- und Kommunalverwaltung, 8*(4), 121–160.

Landfried, C. (2015). Die Wahl der Bundesverfassungsrichter und ihre Folgen für die Legitimität der Verfassungsgerichtsbarkeit. In R. Chr. van Ooyen & M. H. W. Möllers (Eds.), *Handbuch Bundesverfassungsgericht im politischen System* (pp. 369–387, 2nd ed.). Springer VS.

Landfried, C. (2019). Die Verfassungsgerichtsbarkeit als Potential für demokratisches Regieren. In H. M. Heinig & F. Schorkopf (Eds.), *70 Jahre Grundgesetz. In welcher Verfassung ist die Bundesrepublik* (pp. 255–265). Vandenhoeck & Ruprecht.

Lembcke, O. W., & Güpner, M. (2018). Analyse der Landesverfassungsgerichtsbarkeit in vergleichender Absicht. Ein Beitrag zur Typologisierung und Quantifizierung. *ZLVR—Zeitschrift für Landesverfassungsrecht und Landesverwaltungsrecht, 3*(3), 94–104. Retrieved from https://www.zlvr.de/archiv/

Lembcke, O. W., & Pócza, K. (2020). Neue Wege der empirischen Verfassungsgerichtsforschung am Beispiel des Bundesverfassungsgerichts. In W. Reutter (Ed.), *Verfassungsgerichtsbarkeit in Bundesländern. Theoretische Perspektiven, methodische Überlegungen und empirische Befunde* (pp. 77–98). Springer VS.

LVerfGE. (1993ff.). *Entscheidungen der Verfassungsgerichte der Länder.* Herausgegeben von den Mitgliedern der Gerichte. Band 1 bis 25. Walter de Gruyter.

Momper, W. (2005). Grußworte. In H. Sodan (Ed.), *Verfassungsrechtsprechung in und für Berlin. Ansprachen anläßlich des Festaktes am 27. Oktober 2004* (pp. 9–10). Carl Heymanns Verlag.

Momper, W. (2008). Ansprache und Grußworte. In M. Diwell (Ed.), *Chancen, Möglichkeiten und Risiken der Rechtsprechung. Verfassungsgerichtshof des Landes Berlin. Ansprachen anlässlich des Festaktes am 29. November 2007* (pp. 9–12). Carl Heymanns Verlag.

Montesquieu, Charles-Louis de Secondat, Baron de la Brède et de. (1994). *Vom Geist der Gesetze* [1748]. Auswahl, Übersetzung und Einleitung von Kurt Weigand. Reclam.

Nauber, H. (1986). *Das Berliner Parlament. Struktur und Arbeitsweise des Abgeordnetenhauses von Berlin* (5th ed.). Landeszentrale für politische Bildungsarbeit.

o.V. (2007). Gericht ohne Richterin. *die tageszeitung, April* 30/May 1, 2007, p. 22.

o.V. (2008). Ein Präzedenzurteil. *die tageszeitung*, September 22, 2008, p. 2.

Papier, H.-J. (2002). Die Bedeutung der Landesverfassungsgerichtsbarkeit im Verhältnis zur Bundesverfassungsgerichtsbarkeit. In H. Sodan (Ed.), *Zehn Jahre Berliner Verfassungsgerichtsbarkeit. Ansprachen anläßlich des Festaktes am 24. Mai 2002* (pp. 19–34). Carl Heymans.

Papier, H.-J. (2020). Verfassungsgerichtsrechtsprechung und ihre Wirkung auf föderale Einheiten. In Europäisches Zentrum für Föderalismus-Forschung (Ed.), *Jahrbuch des Föderalismus 2020. Föderalismus, Subsidiarität und Regionen in Europa* (pp. 25–33). Nomos.

Parashu, D. (2017). 25 Jahre Berliner Verfassungsgerichtsbarkeit: Eine Würdigung. *Recht und Politik, 52*(1), 83–93.

Pestalozza, C. (1983). Berlin ohne Verfassungsgericht. In C. Starck & K. Stern (Eds.), *Landesverfassungsgerichtsbarkeit. Teilband I: Geschichte, Organisation, Rechtsvergleichung* (pp. 183–230). Nomos.

Pestalozza, C. (1991). *Verfassungsprozeßrecht. Die Verfassungsgerichtsbarkeit des Bundes und der Länder*. C.H. Beck.

Pfennig, G., & Neumann, M. J. (2000). *Verfassung von Berlin* (3rd ed.). Walter de Gruyter.

Plarre, P., & Schulz, B. (2022). "Knast muss Ultima Ratio sein" (Interview). *die tageszeitung*, January 20, 2022, p. 23.

Pócza, K., Dobos, G., & Gyulai, A. (2017). How to measure the strength of judicial decisions? A methodological framework. *German Law Journal, 18*(6), 1557–1586. Retrieved from https://papers.ssrn.com/sol3/papers.cfm?abstract_id=3082168

Reutter, W. (2017). Der Verfassungsgerichtshof des Landes Berlin. In W. Reutter (Ed.), *Landesverfassungsgerichte in der Bundesrepublik Deutschland. Entwicklung—Aufbau—Funktionen* (pp. 77–104). Springer VS.

Reutter, W. (2018). Richterinnen und Richter am Berliner Verfassungsgerichtshof. *LKV—Landes- und Kommunalverwaltung, 25*(11), 489–495.

Reutter, W. (2019). Constitutional adjudication and judicial activism in a German land. *Perspectives on Federalism, 11*(2), 95–125. Retrieved from http://http://www.on-federalism.eu/attachments/331_download.pdf

Reutter, W. (2020a). Verfassungsgerichtsbarkeit in Bundesländern und Justizialisierung—zur Einführung. In W. Reutter (Ed.), *Verfassungsgerichtsbarkeit in Bundesländern. Theoretische Perspektiven, methodische Überlegungen und empirische Befunde* (pp. 1–22). Springer VS.

Reutter, W. (2020b). Verfassungsrichterinnen und Verfassungsrichter: zur personalen Dimension der Verfassungsgerichtsbarkeit in Bundesländern. In W. Reutter (Ed.), *Verfassungsgerichtsbarkeit*

Chapter 3
Democracy, Federalism, and the Rule of Law: Theoretical Perspectives on Constitutional Adjudication in the German States

"Anything goes!" Paul Feyerabend's (1976) methodological credo seems an apt description of political science research on constitutional adjudication and constitutional courts. In any case, the literature on constitutional jurisdiction and constitutional courts can hardly be assigned to a single methodological or theoretical school. It includes quantitative and qualitative studies, institutional descriptions, comparative reports, individual case analyses, interpretive studies, and empirical-analytical explanatory models. And scholars have already examined the breadth of its dimensions: the appointment of justices, deliberation and decision-making processes in courts, the impact of judgments and their consequences for politics and democracy (Glatzmeier, 2019, pp. 107–283). They have focused on questions pertaining to the legitimacy of constitutional courts and constitutional justices, the consequences of judgments, and the ways in which decisions get made. Not surprisingly, their findings vary, as does their theoretical classification of constitutional courts. In the words of Christoph Hönnige (2007, p. 29): "The literature on constitutional courts is extremely heterogeneous and difficult to classify."

Despite this lack of clarity, the case study presented in the previous chapter can be used to identify the factors that shape and explain the state constitutional courts' position, functioning, and impact. In this context, it is necessary to discuss how the states' constitutional jurisdiction can be classified within the democratic constitutional and German-style federalism (Sect. 3.1) and which sociological factors exist to unravel and explain the state constitutional courts' functioning and influence. In the following, I will draw on three central theoretical perspectives: normative-legalistic approaches; behavioral theories, focused on the empirically observable behavior of judges; and institutional studies, dealing with internal structures and decision-making procedures as well as the consequences of constitutional jurisdiction for politics and democracy. The champions of these approaches are therefore focusing on normative preconditions, institutional structures, personal dimensions (including justices' strategic calculations), and the effects of constitutional courts

W. Reutter, *Constitutional Courts in the German States*, Contributions to Political Science, https://doi.org/10.1007/978-3-031-64751-2_3

states, and create the conditions for a pluralistic understanding of the constitution (Chap. 6). They can thus contribute to the "decentralized pluralization of constitutional law" (Gärditz, 2011, p. 46; Brocker, 2021, pp. 9–10).

However, the "separate constitutional spheres" (*getrennte Verfassungsräume*) in the German multilevel system must not be an obstacle to national integrated jurisdiction. The transformation of the state's diversity into the national state's unity must be possible in the area of constitutional jurisdiction. In other words, it must be possible to structure and coordinate (Möstl, 2005, p. 351) the complex "juxtaposition, interpenetration, and superposition" of fundamentally independent constitutional spheres. As Lars Brocker (2021, p. 5) formulates it, following Andreas Voßkuhle (2011, p. 219f.), it must be possible to develop "jurisdictional coherence" in the German and European multi-level system. Brocker (2021, pp. 5–11), for example, mentions the "interpretation of fundamental rights by the Länder in accordance with the Basic Law" or the mutual recognition of judgments (cf. also Franke, 1994) as practically relevant "networking and coherence strategies." Also vital for my study is that Art. 31 of the Basic Law gives federal law precedence over state law. Moreover, Art. 100 (3) of the Basic Law stipulates that the state constitutional courts must obtain a decision of the Federal Constitutional Court if they "intend to deviate from a decision of the Federal Constitutional Court or of the constitutional court of another state in the interpretation of the Basic Law" (Art. 100 (3) GG). It should be noted that the Federal Constitutional Court is "not a second instance above the state constitutional courts, which would be entitled to review the judgments of the state constitutional courts in their entirety" (BVerfGE 60, 175 (208)). Yet despite this limitation, the Federal Constitutional Court declared a total of 283 state laws unconstitutional between 1951 and 2020, i.e., more than 4 per year (Bundesverfassungsgericht, 2021, p. 36). Marcus Höreth (2020, p. 71) has also argued that the rule of law "takes precedence over federalism" when "federal diversity" could endanger legal unity. In this respect, state constitutional courts can promote the tendency toward unitarization inherent in German federalism (Höreth, 2020; for Rhineland-Palatinate, see Brocker & Emmenegger, 2020; Jutzi, 2011).

While state constitutional adjudication tends to be complementary to the principles of the rule of law and federalism, the relationship between constitutional jurisdiction and democracy is fundamentally controversial. Two basic perspectives are to be distinguished: On the one hand, the states' constitutional courts can be understood as the "watchdogs of democracy" (Steinsdorff, 2010). As the supreme guardians of state constitutions, state constitutional courts issue binding decisions in disputes between constitutional bodies, review the constitutionality of ordinary laws, and constitute an independent venue for protecting fundamental rights (Kneip, 2020, pp. 28–29). State constitutional courts can therefore play a "democratic" role (Kneip, 2020) by checking and controlling public power and contributing to the effective enforcement of human rights and freedoms.

On the other hand, some scholars view constitutional courts as a "counter-majority difficulty" (Bickel, 1962, pp. 16–23). They criticize them as "substitute legislators" or "counter-government" (Landfried, 1984). This is because they can declare the decisions of institutions with a democratic mandate—whether parliament or government—unconstitutional, or even null and void. In addition, if constitutional courts are to perform their task of monitoring state power effectively, they must not be subject to democratic control. The tension between non-majoritarian constitutional jurisprudence and majoritarian democracy is evident here, and sometimes manifests itself in conflicts over the role of constitutional courts. Constitutional courts have often had to fight for their status as "supreme guardians of the constitution" through an act of "self-authorization" (Ooyen, 2019, pp. 918–919). This was also true of the Federal Constitutional Court, which, after its inauguration in September 1951, had to assert itself against both the Federal Court of Justice (*Bundesgerichtshof*) and the federal government of the day, in particular its Minister of Justice, Thomas Dehler (FDP).

Yet even apart from the conflict over the Federal Constitutional Court's status at the beginning of the 1950s, the relationship between democracy and constitutional jurisdiction involves a fundamental structural "contradiction." On the one hand, the question has to be addressed: "Where does a small group of jurists get the right to review the decisions of the elected representatives of the people or to interfere in the disputed delimitation of competences between the powers of the state?" (Steinsdorff, 2010, p. 480) Is there, as Winfried Brohm (2001, p. 9) asks polemically, even an "oligarchy in democracy"? Brohm denies that the Federal Constitutional Court has a "state-controlling function" that would result from the Basic Law. On the other hand, there is the question of whether, in democracies, institutions that are not subject to democratic control should have a say in how the state is to be run. The constitutional courts' decisions are not subject to appeal—or at best only under very limited conditions. They concern fundamental political issues and are reached according to functional principles that are difficult to reconcile with the principle of democracy.

By no means do these questions only arise for the Federal Constitutional Court: The constitutional courts of the states are equally subject to them. For the latter, however, the answers are inconsistent. In principle, state constitutional courts possess the same competences that could spark off a judicialization of politics (oppositional right of action in abstract judicial review, disputes between state organs, concrete judicial review, and constitutional complaints) (Hönnige & Gschwend, 2010, p. 509–511; see also Hönnige, 2011; Höreth 2014). However, the scarcity of studies dealing with the constitutional courts' role in the states allows for no clear conclusions to be drawn.

3.2 Social Sciences on Constitutional Courts and Constitutional Adjudication: An Overview

The connection between law and politics in its various forms, which is constitutive for modern democracies, is the subject of social science research on constitutional jurisdiction and judicialization. This research has proven both general and multifacetted. Four approaches that complement each other can be distinguished: (a) research on constitutional jurisdiction, focused on the institution and its effects on

of the court's justices are published only "sporadically" and are not the result of "a general, broad-based social and legal research interest in the systematic connection between constitutional jurisprudence, judges, and politics" (Ooyen & Möllers, 2015, p. 4). So far, legal sociology has not studied state constitutional courts. However, if the 16 state constitutional courts are included in such studies, the methodological problem of the small number of cases can be overcome.

Research on state constitutional courts: Until a few years ago, state constitutional jurisdiction was virtually unexplored *terra incognita* in political science (Reutter, 2017c).[2] Until recently, political scientists published only short surveys (Leunig, 2023, pp. 202–2015), basic descriptions of individual constitutional courts (Lorenz, 2016; Jesse et al., 2014, pp. 62–65; Reutter 2017a), and analyses of selected decisions (Kropp, 1997). Martina Flick is the only scholar to have dealt comprehensively with the structure and influence of state constitutional courts (Flick, 2008, 2009, 2011a, 2011b). Flick has concluded from her research that state constitutional courts have the "potential" to become "important players in state politics" (2011b, p. 286). However, she does not consider the composition of the courts in her analyses, nor does she examine the impact of state constitutional court decisions on state legislatures. Moreover, she tests her hypotheses on a limited database and works with state averages. Without addressing the content or impact of constitutional court decisions, she determines the power of state constitutional courts based on two criteria: formal citizen access and the legally defined jurisdictional profile.

In recent years, however, political science research on state constitutional courts has seen an upswing. This can be traced back to the general re-evaluation of state politics since Germany's reunification and to the AfD's electoral success at the state and federal levels. Both developments have brought the state level to the fore and motivated a variety of studies on state politics in general and state constitutional jurisdiction in particular (Reutter, 2017b, 2022; Thierse, 2020a, 2020b; Lembcke & Güpner, 2018; see also Chap. 8). Oliver W. Lembcke, for example, has presented an "index for measuring the strength of the [Thuringian Constitutional Court's] jurisdiction" (see below). Lembcke (2017, p. 413) uses this index to measure the "restriction of parliamentary room for maneuver by decisions of the Constitutional Court" and, in combination with other findings, arrives at differentiated results. While the Constitutional Court in Thuringia exercised some "restraint [...] vis-à-vis the state government and the state parliament" in disputes between state organs and in reviewing the admissibility of referenda, it gave the legislature "more far-reaching guidelines" in applications for electoral review and in municipal constitutional complaints; in municipal law, it even took on an "innovative role" (Lembcke, 2017, p. 413). On the basis of these and similar studies, it is now possible to perform a general analysis of state constitutional courts' influence on politics (Chap. 7).

[2] For legal research on state constitutional courts, see: Starck & Stern, 1983; Haack, 2010; Reutter, 2017c.

3.3 Explaining Decision-Making in Constitutional Courts

The question of how judges make decisions seems rhetorical in nature. After all, there should be only one standard for judicial rulings: law and order, that is, the rule of law. Only then, according to the underlying assumption, will the above-mentioned constitutional principles of the rule of law and democracy be accommodated. In simple terms, this means: The legislature passes laws, the executive puts them into practice, and the courts apply them in cases of conflict. This is what the textbooks say. And law students learn *ad nauseam* how to proceed in order to subsume a concrete empirical situation under a legal norm, i.e., to apply the latter to the former. This requires not only gathering evidence in order to establish the facts of the case as accurately as possible, but also interpreting the standards to be applied. This is hard enough. Let me give an example. In the past few years, there have been many cases of accidents in which innocent people have been killed in illegally organized car races. Are the drivers of these cars guilty of negligent homicide or of manslaughter? Had they believed the death of others as possible, but trusted in a positive outcome? Or do they at least accept their death? Even if the motives of the racers could be determined in each individual case, the question would still have to be answered as to whether a criterion for a murder (such as "dangerous means" or "low motives") is actually fulfilled in such a case.

This is even more difficult when it comes to constitutional law, which is teeming with terms that require interpretation but are not necessarily easy to pin down. What is the meaning of human dignity? What is freedom? How far does democracy go? When are situations to be treated as equal or must be regarded as unequal? What exactly is the rule of law? These seem to be political rather than legal issues. The Federal Constitutional Court of Germany took the same view in its memorandum on its own status, arguing that it was its task to resolve political disputes by legal means (Statusbericht, 1957). That is also the basis of the dispute between Hans Kelsen (2008) and Carl Schmitt (1996) at the end of the Weimar Republic (Ooyen, 2015), who grappled with whether constitutional jurisprudence is possible at all. In other words, is constitutional jurisprudence always political jurisprudence and therefore impossible? Schmitt concluded that only the President of the Reich—i.e., a political body—could decide such disputes. After all, courts are not supposed to be political, but independent and subject only to the law and the constitution. As with most of the answers that Schmitt gave, he was wrong here too. At the same time, more than a few defenders understand constitutional jurisprudence as a kind of specialized jurisdiction in matters of constitutional law. According to this understanding, interpreting a constitutional norm is nothing more than interpreting a simple law.

This gives rise to three fundamental questions, which political scientists have addressed in this context: What role does the legal basis (in this case, the state constitutions) play in the judges' decision-making? Do social, political, cultural, or other personal factors affect how judges decide? And finally, what role do the institutional conditions play in the decision-making process? That political (and legal) science has developed different answers to each of these questions should come as

Court, voted the way he did because he was "extremely liberal" (Segal & Spaeth, 2002, p. 86). "Simply put", as Segal and Spaeth emphasized (2002, p. 86). The "strategic model" builds on this approach and expands the explanation of judicial behavior. In this concept, it is no longer just the judges' political preferences—"attitudes"—that determine their judgments, but other factors that are ultimately bundled into a utility function (Epstein et al., 2013, pp. 48–50; Epstein & Knight, 1998; Schlögel, 2024). Calculating this utility function includes, for example, the institutional environment, career considerations, and the time that judges spend working. Finally, "interpretivists" attribute judicial behavior to historical and sociological factors (Hönnige, 2011).

Institutionalism: But this view has also found its critics, for two reasons: First, researchers have criticized behavioral approaches for failing to account for the legal and institutional conditions governing judicial behavior. If political preferences, social background, or professional ambitions primarily or even exclusively explain the decisions of constitutional judges, where does that leave the law and the constitution in the decision-making process? Second, one needs to ask whether institutional factors matter—a particularly vital consideration in the present context. After all, the judges of the states' constitutional courts operate in an environment that is legally and politically structured. With Silvia von Steinsdorff (2019, p. 221), this position can be summarized as follows: What matters are less the judges' individual motives, as emphasized by "attitudinalists," but rather the institutional factors—such as advisory routines, practiced procedures—that "predispose, channel, and ultimately also shape the content" of judges' behavior. Mathilde Cohen has argued in a similar vein, distinguishing between ex ante and ex post courts. Cohen sees the American Supreme Court as a paradigmatic ex post court. Its justices have an independent judicial power and are able to express their judgment separately from their colleagues as a "concurring" or "dissenting" opinion. They reach their decisions individually, after joint deliberation. For *ex ante* courts, the opposite is true. The process of these—such as the Federal Constitutional Court, or the constitutional courts of the states—is based on a rapporteur *(Berichterstatter)* who submits a draft decision to the panel of judges for deliberation. From this perspective, the court is a unified body of judges and only the court as a whole makes decisions, even if dissenting votes are possible (Cohen, 2014). In a nutshell, in ex post courts deliberation shapes the decision-making process and precedes it, whereas in ex ante courts deliberation proceeds on the basis of a decision proposed by the judge-rapporteur (see also Ernst, 2012; Andrade, 2020, pp. 61–74; Lübbe-Wolff, 2014, 2023, pp. 22–42).

References

Andrade, M. A. (2020). *Verfassungsgerichtliche Entscheidungsfindung und ihre Folgen: Das Türkische Verfassungsgericht zwischen Mehrheitslogik und Konsensverfahren*. Nomos.

Badura, P. & Dreier, H. (Eds.) (2001). Festschrift 50 Jahre Bundesverfassungsgericht. Band 1: Verfassungsgerichtsbarkeit, Verfassungsprozess. Mohr Siebeck.

Berger, H. (2018). Die Methoden und Entscheidungsprozesse der Landesverfassungsgerichtsbarkeit. *ZLVR—Zeitschrift für Landesverfassungsrecht und Landesverwaltungsrecht, 3*(3), 87–93.

Beyme, K.v. (2001). Das Bundesverfassungsgericht aus der Sicht der Politik- und Gesellschaftswissenschaften. In P. Badura & H. Dreier (Eds.), Festschrift 50 Jahre Bundesverfassungsgericht. *Band 1: Verfassungsgerichtsbarkeit* (pp. 493–505). Mohr Siebeck.

Bickel, A. M. (1962). *The least dangerous branch. The Supreme Court at the Bar of Politics.* Bobbs-Merrill.

Böckenförde, E.-W. (1999). *Staat, Nation, Europa. Studien zur Verfassungslehre, Verfassungstheorie und Rechtsphilosophie*. Suhrkamp.

Boyd, C. L., Epstein, L., & Martin, A. D. (2010). Untangling the causal effects of sex on judging. *American Journal of Political Science, 54*(2), 389–411.

Brocker, L. (2021). Landesverfassungsgerichtsbarkeit(en). Von Verbundstrategien und Gravitationsfeldern. *Die öffentliche Verwaltung, 74*(1), 1–11.

Brocker, L., & Emmenegger, S. (2020). Landesverfassungsgerichtsbarkeit und Verfassungswandel. Entwicklungslinien aus 70 Jahren Verfassungsrechtsprechung in Rheinland-Pfalz. In M. Glaab, H. Hering, M. Kißener, D. Schiffmann, & M. Storm (Eds.), *70 Jahre Rheinland-Pfalz* (pp. 271–286). Springer VS.

Brohm, W. (2001). Die Funktion des BVerfG—Oligarchie in der Demokratie? *Neue Juristische Wochenschrift (NJW), 54*(1), 1–10.

Bryde, B.-O. (1998). Die Verfassungsgerichtsbarkeit in der Rechtssoziologie. In J. Brand & D. Strempel (Eds.), *Soziologie des Rechts. Festschrift für Erhard Blankenburg zum 60. Geburtstag* (pp. 491–504). Nomos.

Bryde, B.-O. (2000). Juristensoziologie. In H. Dreier (Ed.), *Rechtssoziologie am Ende des 20. Jahrhunderts* (pp. 137–155). Mohr Siebeck.

Bundesverfassungsgericht. (2021). *Jahresstatistik 2020.* www.bundesverfassungsgericht.de/DE/Verfahren/Jahresstatistiken/2020/gb2020/Gesamtstatistik%202020.pdf?

Clayton, C. W. (1999). The supreme court and political jurisprudence: New and old institutionalisms. In C. W. Clayton & H. Gillman (Eds.), *Supreme court decision-making. New institutionalist approaches* (pp. 15–41). University of Chicago Press.

Cohen, M. (2014). Ex ante versus ex post deliberations: Two models of judicial deliberations in courts of last resort. *The American Journal of Comparative Law, 62*(4), 951–1008.

Dahl, R. A. (1957). Decision-making in a democracy: The supreme court as a National Policy-Maker. *Journal of Public Law, 6*, 279–295.

Dyevre, A. (2010). Unifiying the field of comparative judicial politics: Towards a general theory of judicial behaviour. *European Political Science Review, 2*(2), 297–327.

Epstein, L., & Knight, J. (1998). *The choices judges make*. CQ.

Epstein, L., & Martin, A. D. (2004). Does age (really) matter? A response to Manning, Carroll and Carp. *Social Science Quarterly, 85*(1), 19–30.

Epstein, L., Knight, J., & Martin, A. D. (2001). The supreme court as a strategic national policy-maker. *Emory Law Journal, 50*, 583–611.

Epstein, L., Landes, W. M., & Posner, R. A. (2013). *The behavior of Federal Judges*. A Theoretical & Empirical Study of Rational Choice.

Ernst, W. (2012). Abstimmen über Rechtserkenntnis. Gedanken zur Entscheidungsfindung in Richterkollegien. *Juristenzeitung, 67*(13), 637–648.

Feyerabend, P. (1976). *Wider den Methodenzwang*. Suhrkamp.

Flick, M. (2008). Landesverfassungsgerichtsbarkeit. In M. Freitag & A. Vatter (Eds.), *Die Demokratien der deutschen Bundesländer. Politische Institutionen im Vergleich* (pp. 237–256). Barbara Budrich.

Flick, M. (2009). Oppositionelle Akteure vor den Landesverfassungsgerichten. *Zeitschrift für Vergleichende Politikwissenschaft, 3*(2), 283–302.

Flick, M. (2011a). Der Einfluss der Landesverfassungsgerichte auf das Parlamentsrecht der deutschen Bundesländer. *Zeitschrift für Parlamentsfragen, 42*(3), 587–603.

Peresie, J. L. (2005). Female judges matter: Gender and Collegial Decisionmaking in the Federal Appellate Courts. *Yale Law Review, 114*(7), 1759–1790.

Pócza, K., Dobos, G., & Gyulai, A. (2017). How to measure the strength of judicial decisions? A methodological framework. *German Law Journal, 18*(6), 1557–1586. Retrieved from https://papers.ssrn.com/sol3/papers.cfm?abstract_id=3082168

Pritchett, C. H. (1948). *The Roosevelt court* (Vol. 47, p. 291). Macmillan.

Rehder, B. (2007). *What is political about jurisprudence: Courts, politics and political science in Europe and the United States*. Discussion Paper 07/5, Köln (MPIfG). Retrieved from https://www.econstor.eu/bitstream/10419/19942/1/dp07-5.pdf

Reutter, W. (Ed.). (2017a). *Landesverfassungsgerichte. Aufgaben—Struktur—Entwicklung*. Springer VS.

Reutter, W. (2017b). Landesverfassungsgerichte in der Bundesrepublik Deutschland — eine politikwissenschaftliche Bestandsaufnahme. In W. Reutter (Ed.), *Landesverfassungsgerichte in der Bundesrepublik Deutschland. Entwicklung—Aufbau—Funktionen* (pp. 21–48). Springer VS.

Reutter, W. (2017c). Der Verfassungsgerichtshof des Landes Berlin. In W. Reutter (Ed.), *Landesverfassungsgerichte in der Bundesrepublik Deutschland. Entwicklung—Aufbau—Funktionen* (pp. 77–104). Springer VS.

Reutter, W. (2018). Landesverfassungsgerichte: "Föderaler Zopf" oder "Vollendung des Rechtsstaates"? *Recht und Politik, 54*(2), 195–207.

Reutter, W. (2020). Verfassungsgerichtsbarkeit in Bundesländern und Justizialisierung—zur Einführung. In W. Reutter (Ed.), *Verfassungsgerichtsbarkeit in Bundesländern. Theoretische Perspektiven, methodische Überlegungen und empirische Befunde* (pp. 1–22). Springer VS.

Reutter, W. (2022). *Landesverfassungsgerichtsbarkeit*. Kohlhammer.

Rottleuthner, H. (1982). Abschied von der Justizforschung. Für eine Rechtssoziologie "mit mehr Recht". *Zeitschrift für Rechtssoziologie, 3*(1), 82–119.

Rottleuthner, H. (1984). Soziale Merkmale, Einstellungen und Verhaltensweisen von Arbeitsrichtern. In H. Rottleuthner (Ed.), *Rechtssoziologische Studien zur Arbeitsgerichtsbarkeit* (pp. 291–297). Nomos.

Schlögel, M. (2024). Strategen in Roben Einflussfaktoren auf die Rechtsprechung des U.S. Supreme Court und deren Implikation für das Bundesverfassungsgericht. In R. Chr. van Ooyen & M.H.W. Möllers (Eds.), *Handbuch Bundesverfassungsgericht im politischen System* (3rd ed.). Springer VS. https://doi.org/10.1007/978-3-658-37532-4_73-1

Schmitt, C. (1996). *Der Hüter der Verfassung* [1931]. (4th ed.). Duncker & Humblot.

Segal, J. A., & Spaeth, H. J. (1993). *The supreme court and the attidudinal model*. Cambridge University Press.

Segal, J. A., & Spaeth, H. J. (2002). *The supreme court and the attitudinal model revisited*. University Press.

Segal, J. A., Epstein, L., Cameron, C. M., & Spaeth, H. J. (1995). Ideological values and the votes of US Supreme-Court-Justices revisited. *Journal of Politics, 57*(4), 812–823.

Sieberer, U. (2006). Strategische Zurückhaltung von Verfassungsgerichten: Gewaltenteilungsvorstellungen und die Grenzen der Justizialisierung. *Zeitschrift für Politikwissenschaft, 16*(4), 1299–1325.

Sodan, H. (2001). Unabhängigkeit und Methodik von Verfassungsrechtsprechung. In Präsident des Verfassungsgerichtshofes des Landes Berlin (Eds.), *Wechsel und Kontinuität im Verfassungsgerichtshof des Landes Berlin* (pp. 21–26). C. Heymanns Verlag.

Starck, C., & Stern, K. (Eds.), *Landesverfassungsgerichtsbarkeit. Teilband I: Geschichte, Organisation, Rechtsvergleichung*. Nomos.

Statusbericht. (1957). Der Status des Bundesverfassungsgerichts. Material—Gutachten, Denkschriften und Stellungnahmen mit einer Einleitung von Gerhard Leibholz. *Jahrbuch des öffentlichen Rechts der Gegenwart (N.F.), 6*, 109–221.

Steinsdorff, S. von (2010). Verfassungsgerichte als Demokratie-Versicherung? Ursachen und Grenzen der wachsenden Bedeutung juristischer Politikkontrolle. In K. H. Schrenk & M. Soldner (Eds.), *Analyse demokratischer Regierungssysteme* (pp. 479–498). Springer VS..

Steinsdorff, S. von (2019). (Verfassungs-)Richterliches Entscheiden. In C. Boulanger, J. Rosenstock, & T. Singelnstein (Eds.), Interdisziplinäre Rechtsforschung. Eine Einführung in die geistes- und sozialwissenschaftliche Befassung mit dem Recht und seiner Praxis (pp. 207–226).

Stern, K. (1983). Einführung. In C. Starck & K. Stern (Eds.), *Landesverfassungsgerichtsbarkeit. Teilband I: Geschichte, Organisation, Rechtsvergleichung* (pp. 1–24). Nomos.

Stone Sweet, A. (1999). Judicialization and the construction of governance. *Comparative Political Studies, 32*(1), 147–184.

Stone Sweet, A. (2000). *Governing with judges. Constitutional politics in Europe*. Oxford University Press.

Stone Sweet, A. (2002). Constitutional courts and parliamentary democracy. *West European Politics, 25*(1), 77–100.

Stüwe, K. (1997). *Die Opposition im Bundestag und das Bundesverfassungsgericht. Das verfassungsgerichtliche Verfahren als Kontrollinstrument der parlamentarischen Minderheit*. Nomos.

Stüwe, K. (2015). Bundesverfassungsgericht und Opposition. In R. Chr. van Ooyen & M. H. W. Möllers (Eds.), *Handbuch Bundesverfassungsgericht im politischen System* (2nd ed., pp. 349–368). Springer VS.

Thierse, S. (2020a). Mobilisierung des Rechts. Organisierte Interessen und Verfassungsbeschwerden vor dem Bundesverfassungsgericht. *Politische Vierteljahresschrift, 61*(3), 553–597.

Thierse, S. (2020b). Sondervoten in Landesverfassungsgerichten. In W. Reutter (Ed.), *Verfassungsgerichtsbarkeit in Bundesländern. Theoretische Perspektiven, methodische Überlegungen und empirische Befunde* (pp. 175–202). Springer VS.

Tsebelis, G. (1995). Veto players and law production in parliamentary democracies. In H. Döring (Ed.), *Parliaments and majority rule in Western Europe* (pp. 83–109). Campus.

Tsebelis, G. (2002). *Veto players. How political institutions work*. University Press.

Voigt, R. (2015). Das Bundesverfassungsgericht in rechtspolitologischer Sicht. In R. Chr. van Ooyen & M. H. W. Möllers (Eds.), *Handbuch Bundesverfassungsgericht im politischen System* (2nd ed., pp. 69–94). Springer VS.

Voßkuhle, A. (2011). Die Landesverfassungsgerichtsbarkeit im föderalen und europäischen Verfassungsgerichtsverbund. *Jahrbuch des öffentlichen Rechts der Gegenwart, 59*, 215–243.

nineteenth century, now understood to be too narrow (Stern, 1983, p. 4). However, the framers adopted organizational ideas from these historical antecedents—especially the linking of the newly established constitutional courts with specialized courts—as well as methods of judicial appointment. Add to this the constitutional courts that were created following German unification.

In addressing the need for differentiation, I am here taking up the conclusions of Wilfried Fiedler (1983). Fiedler examined the emergence of state constitutional jurisdiction after 1945 in the states of the Western occupied zones. He concluded that there is a "difficult diversity of development lines" and that the emergence of state constitutional courts can be understood neither as a "closed, homogeneous process of lawmaking nor as a process that can be clearly defined in time" (Fiedler, 1983, pp. 104 and 105). This is all the more true now, after unification and the creation of seven additional constitutional courts (in Brandenburg, Mecklenburg-Western Pomerania, Saxony, Saxony-Anhalt, Thuringia, Berlin, and Schleswig-Holstein). All in all, this means: It is by no means sufficient to refer to the historical experiences of totalitarianism and dictatorship in order to examine and understand the decision-making processes involved in the establishment and design of constitutional courts in the German states. Other influencing factors must also be considered.

In all this confusion, collating an overview of the emergence of state constitutional courts poses particular challenges. On the one hand, it precludes the possibility of tracing in detail how all 16 currently existing state constitutional courts came to be. This would not only go far beyond my survey's scope but would also result in a mere listing of historical facts and data—even if supplemented by interpretation. In short, each and every case is specific and relevant. On the other hand, analytical effort through generalizing and typifying statements is required precisely because of the lack of clarity and the multi-causal perspective. In the following, I seek to develop a sort of ideal-typical history of the emergence of constitutional jurisdiction in the German states from the varying histories of the establishment of the 16 state constitutional courts. My analysis will include the developments in Saarland, Baden-Württemberg, Berlin, and Schleswig-Holstein, which analysts usually mark as special cases. The three state courts of justice of Baden, Württemberg-Baden, and Württemberg-Hohenzollern, which were dissolved in 1952, I exclude from my study. I have restricted my scope to the states reaching the basic decision, i.e., answering the fundamental question of whether they should set up a constitutional court and make said court part of their political order. The conflicts that arose as they implemented laws concerning the constitutional courts' specific designs I take only marginally into account.

I proceed in my analysis as follows: First, I examine the decisions to create the institution(s), that is, the state constitutional courts. Then, I examine the question of which justices were appointed to the newly created constitutional courts. Theoretically speaking: Does the institutional response match the appropriate personnel response? In other words, was there not only a new jurisdiction for the protection of the constitution and democracy, but also a new judiciary that was politically unencumbered and able and willing to defend the constitution and democracy even when they were in danger?

4.1 "Institutional Response": The Creation of State Constitutional Courts in West Germany and After Unification

As shown in Table 3.1, five state constitutions predated the Basic Law, six were adopted in the 1950s, and the remaining five followed German unification in 1990. Almost all state constitutions provided for the establishment of a constitutional court. The only exception was the Constitution of Schleswig-Holstein, called "State Statute," *(Landessatzung)* which entered into force on January 12th, 1950. Even the Constitution of Berlin of 1950 gave the Berlin House of Representatives *(Abgeordnetenhaus)* the task of passing an implementing law for the Constitutional Court provided for in Article 72. Against this background, it would be an almost heroic undertaking to try to trace the states' constitutional jurisdictions back to a single founding motive, such as the totalitarian experience. The developmental paths are too diverse and the time horizons and periods in which these processes took place are too divergent. In addition, I only have the scope to present and analyze selected aspects of these founding histories here. Of particular relevance are three dimensions that impacted the fundamental decisions on whether a constitutional court should be established: aspects of democracy and constitutional theory; considerations of state and federalism theory; and actors (parties, occupying powers, Western advisors). These causal relationships, which must be supplemented by other factors in individual cases, occurred in specific circumstances and developed their effects in different ways. But I will first look at the exceptions—that is, the states that remained without a constitutional jurisdiction of their own, at least for a longer period of time.

As pointed out, no state must equip itself with a court empowered to review the constitutional conformity of the state's public acts. In fact, not all states have taken a positive stance on the question mentioned at the beginning of this chapter, i.e., whether to set up a constitutional court. In Schleswig-Holstein, the powers to interpret the constitution (or the *Landessatzung* at the time), control norms, and manage other state constitutional disputes were transferred to the Federal Constitutional Court. The Federal Constitutional Court then had to decide on a total of 26 state constitutional disputes based on the assignment of state law in accordance with Article 99 of the Basic Law (Bundesverfassungsgericht, 2021, p. 6). Flick Witzig (2017, p. 371) assumes that this competency transfer to the Federal Constitutional Court was rooted in the "uncertain political circumstances" of the time. Accordingly, in 1949 Schleswig-Holstein's parliament did not adopt a full constitution, but, as mentioned, only a "state statute" (*Landessatzung*) limited to aspects of state organization. But this statute did not provide for a constitutional court. It took almost another six decades before Schleswig-Holstein's state parliament decided, in the context of a comprehensive constitutional reform, that the state's constitutional disputes would no longer be decided by the Federal Constitutional Court according to Article 99 of the Basic Law, but by its own state constitutional court (Flick Witzig, 2017, pp. 371–374; Waack, 2008). The necessary Constitutional Court Law entered

486). Hans Nawiesky, a Bavarian politician and constitutional lawyer, viewed the Bavarian Constitutional Court as a contrast to the recent past (Stern, 1983, p. 4). Fiedler (1983, p. 116) argues that comparable aspirations and anticipations in other constitutional and legislative assemblies were crucial in the fundamental decision to establish a court that could effectively safeguard democracy and the constitution. These courts were not designed as a "countervailing power" to the legislature and executive, nor as a "substitute legislature." As Koch-Baumgarten has correctly observed for the Hessian State Court of Justice (2017, p. 177), the primary concern was to "secure democracy."

However, the founding motives shifted with the Basic Law's entry into force on May 23rd, 1949, and the Federal Constitutional Court's ceremonial opening on September 28th, 1951. The Basic Law transformed German constitutional democracy into a defensive one, and the Federal Constitutional Court was established as an authority to effectively protect it. In debates regarding the establishment of state or constitutional courts in Lower Saxony, Baden-Württemberg, Hamburg, and North Rhine-Westphalia, justifications based on state and federalism theory featured prominently (Meyer & Hönnige, 2017; Obrecht, 2017; Blumenthal, 2017; Thierse & Hohl, 2017). During the Baden-Württemberg state parliament's deliberations on the 1954 State Court of Justice law, several speakers emphasized the State Court's crucial role in upholding the country's constitutional structure. The then Minister of Justice Wolfgang Haußmann, FDP/DVP, declared that the State Court of Justice should prevent a degeneration of democracy and be the keystone in the artful power play of the three public powers. Franz Gog, CDU, similarly underlined its significance. Yet another speaker—Otto Gönnenwein, FDP/DVP—referred to German federalism. He argued that the states' constitutional jurisdiction had become less significant since the Federal Constitutional Court began its activities in September 1951 (Landtag Baden-Württemberg, PlPr. 1/26 of May 12th, 1954, pp. 1264, 1266, and 1267). The emphasis on protecting the constitution and democracy, so strongly championed a few years earlier, was now being replaced by a "pragmatic-legal argument" primarily focused on the "usefulness and necessity of state constitutional jurisdiction" (Fiedler, 1983, p. 118).

According to Hans Markus Heimann (2001, pp. 25–26), historical experiences, particularly those related to the GDR's authoritarian regime, did not significantly influence the relevant debates in the new East German states and Berlin. The evidence here is slightly mixed though: During the first reading of the bill for the Saxon Constitutional Court, Günter Kröber (FDP) emphasized that although the GDR had so-called constitutions, it was never possible to pass laws from the perspective of the classic three-way division of powers and have their constitutionality examined by the courts (Sächsischer Landtag, PlPr. 1/56 of November 19th, 1992, p. 3890). Yet the constitutional and legal deliberations of the newly formed states and Berlin only occasionally cited the GDR's past as a reason for the establishment of constitutional courts. Instead, considerations of the rule of law and federalism theory dominated, and West German role models served as inspiration. The constitutional court's purpose, these deliberations expressed, was to emphasize and complement the statehood of a German state. A few examples may suffice to illustrate the importance of a state constitutional court in the effective application and development of the state constitution. During the debate on the first reading of the Thuringian draft constitution, several speakers emphasized this point. For instance, the CDU's Jörg Schwäblein declared that the state constitutional court would play a role similar to the one the Federal Constitutional Court played for the Basic Law. Additionally, the FDP's Andreas Kniepert noted that the possibility of having administrative acts and laws reviewed by the courts was the democratic state's most important advantage vis à vis the GDR (Landtag Thüringen, PlPr. 1/28 of September 12, 1991, pp. 1710 and 1716). In September 1991, Saxony-Anhalt's argument patterns proved no different. According to Saxony-Anhalt's Minister of Justice Walter Remmers (CDU), the state constitutional jurisdiction was a visible expression of a state's statehood within German federalism (Landtag Sachsen-Anhalt, PlPr. 1/40 of November 12th, 1992, p. 4490; Ulrich Seidel, CDU, PlPr. 1/50 of July 7, 1993, p. 5869, expressed a similar view). Klaus Finkelnburg (CDU), however, relied on constitutional arguments. He viewed the Berlin Constitutional Court as the cornerstone of the constitutional state (Berlin Abgeordnetenhaus, PlPr. 11/40 of September 13th, 1990, p. 2037). From this perspective, constitutional jurisdiction is not merely a response to totalitarianism, but rather an essential element of democracy, the rule of law, and federalism.

In this context, I should mention the role that historical models played in these constitutional deliberations. It is worth noting that the German states' courts could decide disputes between organs, ministerial impeachments, or even violations of fundamental rights long before 1945, as various sources attest (Fiedler, 1983, p. 114f.; Obrecht, 2017, p. 28; Weigl, 2017, p. 53f.; Ketelhut, 2017, pp. 129–132; Blumenthal, 2017, p. 149f.). Bavarian constitutional jurisprudence dates back to its constitution of 1818, which allowed citizens, communities, and estates to file complaints (Title VII § 21, Title X §§ 5 and 6). The Bamberg Constitution of 1919 expanded on this by creating a state court of justice that could decide on ministerial indictments, constitutional complaints, and constitutional disputes for which legal recourse was not available (Article 70). The State Court of Justice was composed of the President of the Bavarian Supreme Regional Court as the chairman, eight judges appointed by the President of the Court or the President of the Supreme Regional Court, and ten additional members elected by the state parliament with a two-thirds majority (Art. 70 (2) Bamberg Constitution of August 14, 1919). An examination of court rulings, laws, or other state sovereign acts was not considered. Such a competence for a court would have been difficult to reconcile with the understanding of the separation of powers that then held sway. The Constitution of the Kingdom of Württemberg from 1819 also contained similar requirements (Obrecht, 2017, p. 28).

In other states, however, a reference to tradition can only be suggested in a general form. This is because most of the states formed after 1945 were largely artificial creations, as noted by Sturm (2015, p. 74), and more original than authentic, as Theodor Heuss, the first President of the Federal Republic of Germany, once remarked (Weichlein, 2019, p. 18). In certain instances, during the constitutional debates after 1945, there were no historical models that could stand for a specific regional tradition. As a result, their references remained general and related to principles of state theory.

other reservations. The SPD and FDP put into question whether North Rhine-Westphalia which was created in 1946, should become a proper state. In consequence, they saw no need for a constitutional court (Dästner, 2002, pp. 14–16). The situation was different in the East German states: No party in any of these states expressed any fundamental opposition to the establishment of a state constitutional court (Heimann, 2001, pp. 28–30). Differences only existed in questions of detail, whereby the LL/PDS—at the time, according to Heimann, seeking to profile itself as the "'guardian of East German interests'"—wanted to define reasons for the exclusion of judges as narrowly as possible and warned that the East German constitutional judiciary could be dominated by West German lawyers (Heimann, 2001, p. 30; cf. Horst Kellner (PDS), Berlin House of Representatives, PlPr. 12/19 of November 28, 1991, p. 1482).

Overall, I have attempted to demonstrate that state constitutional jurisdiction can by no means be traced back monocausally to a single motive or cause. Rather, the conditions and contexts of emergence vary both between the occupation zones and over time. The "anti-totalitarian response" therefore developed its effects in different ways and in many cases was at best indirectly noticeable. Further considerations relate to questions of constitutional, democratic, and federalist theory. From an institutional perspective, constitutional jurisdiction responds to several things: totalitarian or authoritarian experiences, theoretical considerations, historical role models, and constellations of actors (Möllers, 2019, pp. 283–287).

4.2 "Personnel Response": The First Justices in West and East German State Constitutional Courts

New political institutions such as state constitutional courts need politically unencumbered staff. That seems plausible. How could democracy and the rule of law be established and maintained without democrats and democratically minded lawyers? But what may sound plausible as an abstract postulate often turns out to be difficult to implement in constitutional practice. The Federal Constitutional Court provides an apt illustration. As an institutional innovation, it was able to effectively protect democracy and the constitution and at the same time marked a fresh start in terms of personnel, with justices who were professionally qualified and politically unaffected (Ley, 1982; Görtemaker & Safferling, 2016, pp. 288–291). These were apparently requirements that only a few judges met in the early 1950s. In any case, the Federal Constitutional Court as a "belated constitutional body" was only able to begin its activities in Karlsruhe in September 1951 because, among other things, the search for "suitable and widely recognized personalities for the office of justice at this highest court in the young democracy" proved time-consuming and difficult (Ley, 1982, p. 521). As it later turned out, this search was not only extensive, but also did not always lead to the desired result. The majority of the justices of the Federal Constitutional Court elected in 1951 were opponents of National Socialism, had been persecuted in the Third Reich, had returned from emigration after 1945, or had retreated into "internal emigration." However, Rottleuthner (2010, p. 90) reports that 4 of the 24 federal constitutional justices appointed in 1951 had already begun their legal careers before 1945. Not all early constitutional justices, therefore, can be qualified as personally "suitable." Willi Geiger here provides the most notorious and well-known example (Görtemaker & Safferling, 2016, pp. 291–296; Kramer, 1994; see also Balz, 2023). Geiger was a justice at the Federal Constitutional Court for 26 years as well as a judge at the Federal Court of Justice for 10 of those years. He joined the SA and the NSDAP at an early age, justified the dismissal of Jewish journalists and the associated professional bans in his dissertation from 1941, and applied for and enforced several death sentences as a public prosecutor at a special court in Bamberg (1940–1943). Nevertheless, Geiger was classified as "exonerated" in a de-Nazification process and from 1949 onwards, as head of the Ministry of Justice's constitutional department, was able to play a key role in drafting the law on the Federal Constitutional Court, to which he was elected in 1951 and of which he was a member until 1977. Against this background, it seems almost trifling that Geiger—disregarding the confidentiality of deliberations—also continuously informed the Adenauer government about the Federal Constitutional Court's internal processes (Hoffmann, 2000, p. 253).

Based on this history and following the study by Ley (1982), a simple question can be asked: How were the first appointments to the state constitutional courts made? The group of justices in question were supposed to both breathe life into the newly created courts and mark a fresh start. Yet a fundamental problem arises: Relevant studies on this topic are largely missing. Although a number of studies addressing elite change in East Germany have taken the judicial system after 1990 into account, none have analyzed constitutional jurisdiction. Hans-Hubertus von Roenne (1997) examined the practice of transferring GDR judges and prosecutors in the East German states and Berlin. Rosemarie Will (2012) prepared a report for the commission 5/1 of the Brandenburg state parliament on the topic: "Human resources policy in the public service of the state of Brandenburg using the example of personnel changes in the area of judges and public prosecutors." However, neither Will nor von Roenne concerned themselves with how the constitutional courts were filled, but rather with the transfer of legal staff (especially judges and prosecutors) into the service of the states created after 1990. I will nonetheless repeatedly refer to both studies. The state of research on the early constitutional justices in the West German states is even poorer. There now also exist numerous studies on the judges and the judicial system of the early Federal Republic of Germany. They all conclude that for the vast majority of lawyers, the transition from the National Socialist regime to the post-war society of the early Federal Republic of Germany went surprisingly smooth (Raim, 2013; Herbert, 2013). The state constitutional courts play no role in these studies. Only Peter Rütters (2020, p. 103) has examined in an "exploratory and exemplary" way the extent to which selected state constitutional courts were initially characterized and dominated by Nazi-influenced justices. For the remainder of this presentation, I am taking up the central findings from Rütters' analysis and supplementing them if possible. In addition, I have conducted an intertemporal comparison between the post-war and post-reunification phases,

In addition, the de-Nazification procedures carried out by the occupying powers, which were continued by German tribunals from 1947 onwards, were not very effective. Those associated with, or had been part of, the Nazi regime found them to be small barriers to their own reintegration into the judicial service after 1949. Similarly, the "Regulation of the Legal Relationships of the Persons Covered by Article 131 of the Basic Law" *(Regelung der Rechtsverhältnisse der unter Artikel 131 des Grundgesetzes fallenden Personen)* of April 10th, 1951, known by some as the "Denazification Final Act" *(Entnazifizierungs schlussgesetz),* allowed many jurists associated with the Nazis to return to their previous or comparable positions (Rütters, 2020, p. 148). Ulrich Herbert also credits former Nazi jurists with extraordinary success in this regard. They almost all completely succeeded in securing corresponding positions and offices in the newly created Federal Republic of Germany of the 1950s. In the decades after the war, the Nazi regime's former partisans "significantly" determined the Federal Republic's judicial system (Herbert, 2013, p. 54). According to Rütters' findings, the state constitutional courts proved no exception. Here, too, a considerable number of appointed justices demonstrated continuity across systems (Rütters, 2020, p. 103). Many had already begun their legal careers between 1933 and 1945 and carried them on with almost no interruption after the Federal Republic of Germany's founding and the adoption of the abovementioned "Denazification Final Act."

This was fundamentally different in the East German states, both with regard to the judiciary in general and the constitutional justices in particular. The People's Chamber *(Volkskammer)*, elected on March 18th, 1990, had already passed regulations in June 1990 on how to deal with judges and prosecutors who had previously served in the GDR, and the unification treaty and the states that joined the scope of the Basic Law in 1990 followed them. The plan was to carry out a general review of all judges and prosecutors who, according to the agreement, were allowed to remain in their positions for a limited period of time and eventually could be taken over if they filed a respective request. Committees at the state ministries of justice examined these applications, and the ministers of justice generally followed their recommendations. The decision was made on the basis of a catalog of criteria—which, however, varied between the states. Berlin refused to take on or hire (above the district level) any judges or public prosecutors who had worked in political criminal law in the GDR, who had been employees of the Ministry for State Security, who had held management positions in the SED or had been high-ranking officials in the GDR (Will, 2012, pp. 37–40; Roenne, 1997, pp. 91–119). It was undisputed that, as stipulated in the unification agreement of August 31st, 1990, the "diploma in law" degree *(Diplomjurist)* acquired in the GDR should qualify for judicial office according to the German Judiciary Act *(Deutsches Richtergesetz).* The transition therefore dispensed with the usual "selection of the best" and a technical examination of the applicants. Only one criterion should mandate exclusion from the transition process—"objective intolerability." This meant that "anyone who could be seen as too burdensome in the eyes of the population could not be taken on to build a constitutional state" (Will, 2012, p. 38). Berlin alone made an exception, as the judges and prosecutors in the city's eastern part were dismissed and had to reapply on the basis of the German Judiciary Act.

According to H. H. von Roenne, 1780 judges were working in the then five new states and East Berlin at the end of 1989. Of these, 366 left and 1414 applied for a job, of which 681 were taken on as probationary judges—meaning that a total of 382 judges were rejected (Roenne, 1997, p. 312) and that around 38% of all judges working in the GDR were taken over into the Federal Republic of Germany's civil service or judicial system. In her report to the state parliament, Rosemarie Will comes to an overall positive assessment of the procedures she reviewed in Brandenburg. The judges and public prosecutors who were transferred in this state, she laid out in a hearing in the Brandenburg state parliament, had "an extraordinarily precise and democratically legitimized procedure according to the rule of law" (Landtag Brandenburg, Protokoll Enquete-Kommission 5/18 from February 17th, 2012, p. 18). H. H. von Roenne (1997, p. 271) also assesses the procedure and result of the transfer of judges and prosecutors in the five new states and Berlin as overall "successful." The constitutional state has come to terms with its "pre-constitutional past," although employees from the former GDR remained in the minority in the judicial system that was rebuilt after 1990. It should also be taken into account that rejected applicants—in contrast to other professional groups—"were not threatened with unemployment" because they found new job opportunities (Roenne, 1997, p. 271).

Constitutional justices were not directly exposed to such scrutiny when they were elected. Nevertheless, they had to meet the eligibility requirements, which in Mecklenburg-Western Pomerania, Saxony, and Saxony-Anhalt included, among other things, that "anyone who violates the principles of humanity or the rule of law could not be elected to the respective state constitutional court" and cannot have worked for the "Ministry for State Security/Office for National Security of the GDR" (§ 3 (4) LVerfGG MW). In Thuringia, a justice can be removed from office if he or she "knowingly worked as a full-time or unofficial employee with the Ministry for State Security, the Office for National Security, or representatives of these institutions" (§ 6 (2) No. 3 ThürVerfGHG). With the exception of Brandenburg, constitutional court laws have already excluded electoral eligibility for the reasons mentioned (violation of the principles of humanity or the rule of law; full-time or unofficial employee within the meaning of § 6 (4) of the Stasi Documents Act). These facts also constitute grounds for a constitutional justice's dismissal (§§ 6 and 11 VerfGGLSAT; §§ 2 and 6; §§ 3 and 6 LVerfGG MW). The only place this regulation met with controversy was in the discussions of Saxony's state parliament, where the PDS insisted on an individual case review—one that was, in any case, already mandatory. Upon appointment, a constitutional justice must additionally take an oath to the state constitution—and in some cases the Basic Law—in which they naturally also swear to "serve only the truth and justice" (§ 5 (2) VerfGGBbg). It therefore remained incumbent upon the state parliament to check (in the course of an election process and possibly with a request to the Stasi records authority *[Stasiunterlagenbehörde]*) whether proposed candidates were sufficiently qualified and personally suitable for office. Overall, this means that the legal regulations and their underpinning review procedures were much more detailed in the East German states after reunification than in the West German states after the Second World War and fascism. As pointed out the parliaments and the ministries carried out a complete review of all East German judges before taking them on into the judicial system.

In addition to the legal measures mentioned, Rütters (2020, p. 108) cites "organizational regulations" aimed at neutralizing and containing the possible influence of

average age when assuming office was higher in older West German constitutional courts than in those established after 1990, although both groups display variances and I could not determine the age for all justices. In the younger constitutional courts, the early justices were on average almost 52 years old; their West German colleagues, who were elected around four decades earlier, were around 3 years older, and in Baden-Württemberg they were on average almost 60. The first generation of justices of the state constitutional courts established in the 1940s and 1950s was therefore predominantly politically socialized in the Weimar Republic, while that of the East German states was shaped by the 1960s. In general, justices at constitutional courts are on average almost 53 years old when they take office, and the first generation of justices fits this pattern (see Chap. 6).

The average proportion of professional judges in the older state constitutional courts is just under 60%, significantly higher than in the courts created after reunification, where it lies at around 48%. The proportion of female justices in the courts that were established later is also significantly higher, reaching an average of over 21%. All constitutional courts created after 1990 had at least one woman in the founding generation; at the Berlin Constitutional Court and the Brandenburg State Constitutional Court there were even three—as required by law. Things were fundamentally different in the 1940s and 1950s. After 1945, the early constitutional courts in West German states were purely male bastions. Amongst the 97 justices who took office between June 4th, 1947, and January 27th, 1959, there was just one woman.

Overall, the intertemporal comparison brings some differences to the fore, but these can only partially be attributed to considerations of democratic theory. Only the constitutional courts in the East German states created after 1990 can claim to have offered not only institutional innovation, but also fresh starts in terms of personnel.

References

Balz, E. (2023). Biographien in Graustufen. Die ersten 24 Richter am Bundesverfassungsgericht und ihre Erfahrungen in der NS-Zeit. In R. van Ooyen & M. Möllers (Eds.), *Handbuch Bundesverfassungsgericht im politischen System* (3rd ed.). Springer VS. https://doi.org/10.1007/978-3-658-37532-4_14-1

Blumenthal, J. von (2017). Das Hamburgische Verfassungsgericht. In W. Reutter (Ed.), Landesverfassungsgerichte. Entwicklung—Aufbau—Funktionen (pp. 149–174). Springer VS.

Bundesverfassungsgericht (2021). *Jahresstatistik 2020*. www.bundesverfassungsgericht.de/DE/Verfahren/Jahresstatistiken/2020/gb2020/Gesamtstatistik%202020.pdf?

Dästner, C. (2002). Die Entstehung und Entwicklung der nordrhein-westfälischen Verfassungsgerichtsbarkeit. In Präsident des Verfassungsgerichtshofs für das Land Nordrhein-Westfalen (Ed.), *Verfassungsgerichtsbarkeit in Nordrhein-Westfalen. Festschrift zum 50-jährigen Bestehen des Verfassungsgerichtshofs für Land Nordrhein-Westfalen (pp. 13–31).*

Ewert, S., & Hein, M. (2017). Das Landesverfassungsgericht Mecklenburg-Vorpommern. In W. Reutter (Ed.), *Landesverfassungsgerichte. Entwicklung—Aufbau—Funktionen* (pp. 199–218). Springer VS.

Fiedler, W. (1983). Die Entstehung der Landesverfassungsgerichtsbarkeit nach dem Zweiten Weltkrieg. In C. Starck & K. Stern (Eds.), *Landesverfassungsgerichtsbarkeit.*

Teilband I: Geschichte, Organisation, Rechtsvergleichung. Studien und Materialien zur Verfassungsgerichtsbarkeit (pp. 104–153). Nomos.

Finkelnburg, K. (2001). Die ersten acht Jahre des Verfassungsgerichtshofes des Landes Berlin. In Präsident des Verfassungsgerichtshofes des Landes Berlin (Ed.), *Wechsel und Kontinuität im Verfassungsgerichtshof des Landes Berlin. Ansprachen anläßlich des Festaktes am 14. April 2000* (pp. 13–20). Carl Heymanns Verlag.

Flick Witzig, M. (2017). Das Schleswig-Holsteinische Landesverfassungsgericht. In W. Reutter (Ed.), *Landesverfassungsgerichte. Entwicklung—Aufbau—Funktionen* (pp. 371–388). Springer VS.

Görtemaker, M., & Safferling, C. (2016). *Die Akte Rosenburg. Das Bundesministerium der Justiz und die NS-Zeit*. C.H. Beck.

Heimann, H. M. (2001). *Die Entstehung der Verfassungsgerichtsbarkeit in den neuen Ländern und in Berlin*. Verlag Franz Vahlen.

Herbert, U. (2013). Justiz und NS-Vergangenheit in der Bundesrepublik 1945-1970. In M. Görtemaker & C. Safferling (Eds.), *Die Rosenburg. Das Bundesministerium der Justiz und die NS-Vergangenheit—eine Bestandsaufnahme* (pp. 43–59). Vandenhoeck & Ruprecht.

Hoffmann, D. (2000). Das Bundesverfassungsgericht im politischen Kräftefeld der frühen Bundesrepublik. Die Auseinandersetzung um die Westverträge 1952-1954. *Historisches Jahrbuch, 120*, 227–273.

Ketelhut, J. (2017). Verfassungsgerichtsbarkeit im Zwei-Städte-Staat. Der Staatsgerichtshof der Freien Hansestadt Bremen. In W. Reutter (Ed.), *Landesverfassungsgerichte. Entwicklung—Aufbau—Funktionen* (pp. 129–148). Springer VS.

Koch-Baumgarten, S. (2017). Der Staatsgerichtshof in Hessen zwischen unitarischem Bundesstaat, Mehrebenensystem und Landespolitik. In W. Reutter (Ed.), *Landesverfassungsgerichte. Entwicklung—Aufbau—Funktionen* (pp. 175–198). Springer VS.

Kramer, H. (1994). Ein vielseitiger Jurist. Willi Geiger (1909-1994). *Kritische Justiz, 27*(2), 232–237.

Lembcke, O. W. (2017). Thüringer Verfassungsgerichtshof. In W. Reutter (Ed.), *Landesverfassungsgerichte. Entwicklung—Aufbau—Funktionen* (pp. 389–420). Springer VS.

Ley, R. (1982). Die Erstbesetzung des Bundesverfassungsgerichtes. *Zeitschrift für Parlamentsfragen, 13*(4), 521–541.

Lorenz, A. (2017). Das Verfassungsgericht Brandenburg als politisiertes Organ? Möglichkeiten und Grenzen politischer Einflussnahme. In W. Reutter (Ed.), *Landesverfassungsgerichte. Entwicklung—Aufbau—Funktionen* (pp. 105–128). Springer VS.

Meyer, P., & Hönnige, C. (2017). Der Niedersächsische Staatsgerichtshof. In W. Reutter (Ed.), *Landesverfassungsgerichte. Entwicklung—Aufbau—Funktionen* (pp. 219–242). Springer VS.

Möllers, C. (2019). Legalität, Legitimität und Legitimation des Bundesverfassungsgerichts. In M. Jestaedt, O. Lepsius, C. Möllers, & C. Schönberger (Eds.), *Das entgrenzte Gericht. Eine kritische Bilanz nach sechzig Jahren Bundesverfassungsgericht* (pp. 281–422, 3rd ed.). Suhrkamp.

Obrecht, M. (2017). Verfassungsgerichtshof Baden-Württemberg. In W. Reutter (Ed.), *Landesverfassungsgerichte. Entwicklung—Aufbau—Funktionen* (pp. 27–52). Springer VS.

Pestalozza, C. (1983). Berlin ohne Verfassungsgericht. In C. Starck & K. Stern (Eds.), *Landesverfassungsgerichtsbarkeit. Teilband I. Geschichte, Organisation, Rechtsvergleichung* (pp. 183–230). Nomos.

Raim, E. (2013). *Justiz zwischen Diktatur und Demokratie. Wiederaufbau und Ahndung von NS-Verbrechen in Westdeutschland 1945–1949*. Oldenbourg Verlag.

Renzsch, W., & Schlüter, K. (2017). Das Landesverfassungsgericht von Sachsen-Anhalt. In W. Reutter (Ed.), *Landesverfassungsgerichte. Entwicklung—Aufbau—Funktionen* (pp. 347–370). Springer VS.

Reutter, W. (2017). Der Verfassungsgerichtshof des Landes Berlin. In W. Reutter (Ed.), *Landesverfassungsgerichte in der Bundesrepublik Deutschland. Entwicklung—Aufbau—Funktionen* (pp. 77–104). Springer VS.

constitution and supplementary regulations "are determined autonomously in the rules of procedure." Undergirding this formal legal provision is the assumption that constitutional bodies are the highest institutions of the state that effectively participate in its management. In this function they enjoy independence from the other constitutional bodies (Starck, 1983, p. 155f.). In its status memorandum of 1952, the Federal Constitutional Court declared that the court, as the "supreme guardian of the constitution [...] according to the letter and spirit of the Basic Law and the Law on the Federal Constitutional Court, is at the same time a constitutional body endowed with the highest authority" (Statusbericht, 1957, p. 144).[1] The Federal Constitutional Court alone has to deal with legal disputes in "which political law is disputed and the political itself becomes the subject of the judicial assessment on the basis of existing norms" (Statusbericht, 1957, p. 145). As in state parliaments and state governments, the state quality of the states manifests in a special way in state constitutional courts.[2]

Against this background, it is surprising that questions relating to the status of the state constitutional courts and their administration "are generally still neglected" (Wittreck, 2006, p. 496f.). Exceptions only confirm the rule (Wittreck, 2006, pp. 493–518; Starck, 1983; Reutter, 2017a, pp. 13–25; Flick, 2011, pp. 17–76). Above all, empirically supported studies that compare the status, administrative structures, and competence profiles of state constitutional courts are largely missing. To what extent is the state constitutional courts' postulated status as a constitutional body legally adequate and with points of reference in state practice? That question has so far remained unanswered.

I will be presenting an answer to this question from an empirical perspective in the following sections, and making two things clear: On the one hand, the states' various constitutional courts differ significantly in terms of legal basis, administrative structure, and budgetary law. These findings do not call into question such courts' status as constitutional bodies, but they do problematize the assumption that they display a "high degree of homogeneity" (Flick, 2011, p. 59). Across the states, the respective state constitutional courts' formal statuses, court administrations, and competence profiles do not guarantee in the same way and to the same extent the degree of independence which is necessary for effective constitutional control of politics, and which the Federal Constitutional Court assumed in its status memorandum (Leibholz, 1957, pp. 110–113).

5.1 State Constitutional Courts as Constitutional Bodies

The story of how the Federal Constitutional Court managed to proclaim and implement its status as a constitutional body has been told many times (Lembcke, 2015; Statusbericht, 1957, Häußler, 1994, pp. 23–29). In contrast, the status of state

[1] The most important documents on the so-called status dispute of the Federal Constitutional Court are published in: JöR (NF), 6 (1957), pp. 109–221 (= Statusbericht, 1957).

[2] I have based the rest of my presentation here on considerations that I have already published elsewhere; see Reutter (2017a).

constitutional courts has so far attracted little academic attention and provoked little political controversy (Starck, 1983; Wittreck, 2006, pp. 493–518). As at the federal level, constitutional jurisdiction in the states rests on a legal triad, consisting of a constitutional basis, simple legal standards (the constitutional court laws), and the rules of procedure that the state constitutional courts give themselves. But that is where the similarities end. The state constitutions already assign varying importance to the highest court in the states. Although all state constitutions have their own sections on state governments and state parliaments, only every second one contains a section on the state constitutional court itself (Table 5.1). Eight state constitutions relegate the provisions regarding their respective highest court to the section on the administration of justice. Only three state constitutions refer to the state constitutional court as "independent" and an "independent court."

Nor do the constitutional court laws close this gap in all states: Only seven actually include the formulation known and already quoted from the Federal Constitutional Court Law that the Constitutional Court is "independent and an

Table 5.1 State Constitutional Jurisdiction in State Constitutions, in Constitutional Court Laws, and in Rules of Procedure of the State Parliaments[a]

	Constitution	Chapter in constitution (Art.)	Status	Number of justices	Deputy	Composition	Right to propose candidates	Majority requirement
BW	1953	— (68)	–	SC	CCL	SC	RoP	CCL
BAV	1947	Yes (60–69)	–	SC	CCL	SC	RoP	RoP
BER	1992	— (84)	CCL	SC	–	SC	RoP	SC
BB	1993	— (112–114)	SC	SC	–	SC	RoP	SC
BRE	1949	— (139–140)	CCL	SC	CCL	SC	RoP	CCL
HAM	1953	— (65)	–	SC	SC	SC	SC/CCL	CCL
HES	1948	Yes (130–133)	CCL	SC	CCL	SC	CCL	CCL
MW	1995	Yes (52–54)	SC	SC	SC	SC	SC/CCL	SC
LS	1957	— (54–55)	CCL	SC	SC	CCL	CCL /RoP	SC
NRW	1952	Yes (75–76)	CCL	SC	SC	SC	RoP	SC
RP	1947	Yes (130–136)	–	SC	SC	SC	SC/CCL	SC
SLD	1959	Yes (96–97)	–	SC	SC	CCL	CCL	SC
SAY	1993	— (81)	–	SC	CCL	SC	CCL	SC
SAT	1993	Yes (74–76)	CCL	SC	SC	CCL	CCL /RoP	SC
SH	2008	— (51)	CCL	SC	CCL	SC	GE/RoP	SC
TH	1995	Yes (79–80)	SC	SC	CCL	SC	RoP	SC

[a] Legal basis for corresponding regulation, whereby: CCA = Constitutional Court Law *(Landesverfassungsgerichtsgesetz)*; SC = state constitution (*Landesverfassung*); RoP = Rules of Procedure of the State Parliament *(Geschäftsordnung Landesparlament)*

Sources: self-compiled; state constitutions, state constitutional court laws, rules of procedure of the state parliaments

in the meantime drawn the right conclusion and granted the constitutional courts "extensive autonomy" in the preparation and execution of their budgets.

It should be noted that the financial resources allocated to state constitutional courts are hardly relevant. In 2016, the budgets of the courts ranged from 24,500 and 843,700 euros—negligible sums in relation to the overall state budgets. In two states the constitutional courts' budgets are even part of the Ministry of Justice.[3] Although it does not follow that a state constitutional court is subject to the Ministry of Justice's supervision, budgetary independence is not fully guaranteed in these cases. Consequently, Hofmann (2018, p. 1167) finds that the Constitutional Court of Baden-Württemberg received an independent individual plan in 2015/16 and is no longer part of the State Ministry. Since then, its President of the Constitutional Court, like the state parliament and the Court of Auditors, has been able to draw up a "counter-budget" and independently negotiate its financing with the state parliament. In addition, five constitutional courts have no administrative support, so it remains unclear who, exactly, is to make up the "auxiliary staff" that should be drawing up the budget and managing funds.

For Wittreck (2006, p. 511f.), the personnel sovereignty (*Personalhoheit*) of the constitutional courts is also "restricted". For Starck (1983, pp. 168–170), an organizational link between a constitutional court and another court also carries the risk that the constitutional court's personnel sovereignty could be encroached upon. A distinction must be made between professional judges and non-professional judges who have been assigned or belong to the constitutional courts.

- Position of the constitutional justices: The Federal Constitutional Court's status memorandum is unequivocal in this respect. Its own constitutional justices cannot qualify as civil servants in the usual sense; they are not subject to the disciplinary and personnel law regulations applicable to civil servants and judges (Statusbericht, 1957). This concept cannot be applied to justices on state constitutional courts. All constitutional court laws stipulate that the office as a constitutional justice has priority over full-time work. However, state constitutional justices work on a honorary basis, so they do not have their own official status as constitutional justices and are therefore only subject to the provisions of the German Judiciary Act to a limited extent and only if the state has created the respective legal requirements (Wittreck, 2006, p. 506). Yet this does not change that the Ministry of Justice retains official supervision over professional judges—though supervision that cannot, of course, extend to their work as constitutional justice. This also applies analogously to university professors who, as civil servants, are additionally assigned to other institutions

[3] In the past, the constitutional courts were usually assigned to other departments anyway. According to Starck (1983, p. 166), the practice at the beginning of the 1980s was that the budget of the Constitutional Court "was assigned to the court where the Constitutional Court was formed" (as in Bavaria, Bremen, and Rhineland-Palatinate), or "was located at the State Chancellery or directly at the Minister of Justice" (as in Baden-Württemberg, Hamburg, Lower Saxony, North Rhine-Westphalia, and Saarland).

under public law. Moreover, in Bavaria, Hamburg, and Rhineland-Palatinate, the president of the state constitutional court is also chairman of the higher administrative or higher regional court (Wittreck, 2006, p. 498), and this personal union can make the Ministry of Justice influence on constitutional jurisprudence at least a theoretical possibility. But here, too, there is no evidence of such influence in practice.

- Administrative Staff: According to Fabian Wittreck (2006, p. 509), the administration of the state constitutional courts is "only fragmentarily regulated in the relevant laws." The president is usually entrusted with this task, sometimes in consultation with the plenary session of justices. An exception is Bavaria, whose Constitutional Court has a full-time Secretary General responsible only for administrative matters. But there is also a full-time head of administration at the Constitutional Court in Berlin, although its role is only provided for in budgetary law and is not, as in Bavaria, determined by the law on the constitutional court. Wittreck (2006, p. 511) assumes a "limited personnel sovereignty," since the "access of the state constitutional courts to the selection and guidance of the staff working to support them [...] is comparatively weak." The constitutional courts are mostly "staffed" by the state judicial administrations. In addition, the supervision of a court's non-judicial staff does not lie with its president (Wittreck, 2006, p. 511–514).

These personnel and legal dimensions correspond to the state constitutional courts' functioning, which differs fundamentally from that of the Federal Constitutional Court. The state constitutional courts decide in plenum—i.e., with the full assembly of justices (the only exception being the Bavarian Constitutional Court with its three panels)—and make most decisions by resolution *(Beschluss)*—i.e., without prior hearing of those involved in the proceedings (Reutter, 2017a, p. 14f.; 2017b, p. 92). Apart from the possibility of rejecting inadmissible or obviously unfounded constitutional complaints through chambers set up for this purpose, it is important in this context that constitutional courts are not permanent institutions. The plenum of the Berlin Constitutional Court meets on average once a month (Reutter, 2017b, p. 91f.), a frequency the other constitutional courts, with their significantly lower workloads, fall far short of reaching. Constitutional justices therefore work in a discontinuous manner, which does not exclude an organ characteristic, but does modify it functionally and structurally.

These findings cannot call into question the state constitutional courts' status as constitutional bodies as such. But they do show that this status takes different forms. Taking all legal foundations, administrative structural conditions, and functioning into account, the state constitutional courts' status as a constitutional body must be defined as "modified," a qualification underpinned by their competences.

the state constitutional courts vary significantly and lend the courts specific profiles (Table 5.4). Notably, although the constitutional courts of the East German states have similar jurisdictional scopes and have existed for a similar length of time, their case numbers fluctuate widely: between 231 (Mecklenburg-Western Pomerania) and 2418 (Saxony) (Ewert & Hein, 2017; Patzelt, 2017). The Berlin Constitutional Court records the most entries per year, while Schleswig-Holstein brings up the rear (Reutter, 2017a; Flick Witzig, 2017). In addition, the caseload of some constitutional courts has tended to increase over time (Glaab, 2017, p. 281; Reutter, 2017b, pp. 89–92; Blumenthal, 2017, pp. 158–166), while that of others has remained near the original level, albeit with fluctuations (Obrecht, 2017, pp. 35–37; Weigl, 2017, pp. 64–67; Lorenz, 2017, pp. 119–122; Ketelhut, 2017, pp. 143–145; Meyer & Hönnige, 2017, pp. 230–234; Renzsch & Schlüter, 2017, pp. 336–262; Rütters, 2017, pp. 309–318). Finally, in six state constitutional courts three out of four submissions are constitutional complaints, while in three such courts municipal constitutional complaints make up the majority of proceedings.

The constitutional courts' relationship to other constitutional bodies can be described in three ideal-typical roles: First, constitutional courts act as "dispute mediators" *(Streitschlichter)* when they decide conflicts between constitutional bodies and answer questions about a state's political order. In this respect, state constitutional courts operate in the area of classic state jurisdiction (Hoke, 1983). The most important procedure in this regard is the *Organstreit* proceeding, organ dispute procedure (Bethge, 1983), which, according to Martina Flick (2011, p. 77), can be classified as a "highly political" one (see also Flick, 2008). However, on average only one in every 50 proceedings falls into this area.

Secondly, state constitutional courts act as "*negative Gesetzgeber*", "negative legislators" (Kelsen, 2008) when they not only apply law but also create it—even if this is only done in a negative way by invalidating a law as unconstitutional. State constitutional courts primarily perform this task in the context of abstract and concrete judicial reviews, in *Popularklagen* (Ulsamer, 1983) and municipal constitutional complaints (Obrecht, 2020; Hildebrandt, 2020; Renzsch, 2020). As part of such proceedings, state constitutional courts can declare laws passed by the state parliament to be unconstitutional. They thus have a political impact—albeit in a negative form. In contrast to the federal level, the states rarely engage judicial reviews. Specialist courts only submit a law to the state constitutional courts for review in exceptional cases. Abstract judicial reviews are initiated only slightly more frequently. The sole exception in this regard is Bavaria, where almost 1500 popular lawsuits *(Popularklagen)* have been filed since 1947, of which around 11% were successful (Weigl, 2017, p. 67). As part of such proceedings, the courts have repeatedly made crucial—sometimes even spectacular—decisions, such as declaring the 2002/03 budget of the state of Berlin unconstitutional or striking down the 2010 budget of the red-green minority government in North Rhine-Westphalia (Thierse & Hohl, 2017, p. 254). In Hesse, judicial reviews have often served to settle fundamental political disputes, as in the fields of education and university policy (Koch-Baumgarten, 2017, p. 188 f.). Yet such cases remain extremely rare, indicating that state constitutional courts have never developed into "substitute legislatures" or *Ersatzgesetzgeber.* It remains the responsibility of the executive and legislative branches to politically shape the states' policies. Still, researchers have

Table 5.4 State Constitutional Courts: Number of Cases by Type (in Percent and Absolute Numbers; Varying Periods)

	Years	Individual constitutional complaints	Disputes between state organs	Concrete judicial reviews	Abstract judicial reviews	Constitutional complaints by municipalities	Others	Number of cases (abs.)[a]	
	(abs.)	(%)	(%)	(%)	(%)	(%)	(%)	(abs.)	(Per year)
BW	60	23.0	8.6	4.7	2.3	46.3	15.2	257	4.3
BAV	68	82.6	0.6	0.0	15.2[b]	0.0	1.5	9.367	137.8
BER	23	95.4	1.5	0.0	0.2	0.0	2.8	4.150	180.4
BB	22	55.2	1.5	0.3	0.4	20.3	22.3[c]	1.908	86.7
BRE	65	0.0	21.4	3.6	20.2	0.0	54.8[d]	84	1.3
HAM	63	0.0	4.2	1.6[e]	0.0	0.0	94.2[f]	190	3.0
HES[g]	66	81.1	1.8	0.0	6.4	0.9	9.8	856	13.0
MW	20	51.1	20.3	0.4	1.3	26.8	0.0	231	11.6
NO	59	0.0	11.6	1.6	7.9	55.3	23.7	190	3.2
NRW	63	0.0	14.2	0.0	3.7	60.8	21.3	431	6.8
RP	22	92.6	1.5[h]	–	–	4.7	0.0	718	32.6
SLD	55	61.1	7.4	2.2	2.6	10.0	16.6	229	4.2
SAY	22	85.8	4.1	0.2	0.6	8.1	1.2	2.418	109.9
SAT	22	40.0	1.8	0.7	0.4	54.3	2.8	562	25.5
SH	7	–	8.3	16.7	25.0	8.3	41.7	12	1.7
TH	20	85.2	2.3	0.7	2.3	8.2	1.2	596	29.8
All	657	77.6	2.2	0.4	7.2	6.8	5.7	22.199	33.8

[a] Different periods and thus different number of cases compared to Table 1.1
[b] Only popular lawsuits *(Popularklagen)*
[c] Including 418 applications for interim measures
[d] Including 20 interpretation procedures and 20 election verification procedures
[e] Concrete and abstract judicial reviews
[f] Including 21 election complaints, 29 challenges to district elections, 22 interim orders and 19 declaratory proceedings
[g] My calculations based on the information in Koch-Baumgarten
[h] Dispute between state organs, concrete and abstract judicial reviews
Sources: self-calculated; Reutter (2017a, p. 19); own additions

Ewert, S., & Hein, M. (2017). Das Landesverfassungsgericht Mecklenburg-Vorpommern. In W. Reutter (Ed.), *Landesverfassungsgerichte. Entwicklung—Aufbau—Funktionen* (pp. 199–218). Springer VS.

Flick, M. (2008). Landesverfassungsgerichtsbarkeit. In M. Freitag & A. Vatter (Eds.), *Die Demokratien der deutschen Bundesländer. Politische Institutionen im Vergleich* (pp. 237–256). Barbara Budrich.

Flick, M. (2011). *Organstreitverfahren vor den Landesverfassungsgerichten. Eine politikwissenschaftliche Untersuchung*. Peter Lang.

Flick Witzig, M. (2017). Das Schleswig-Holsteinische Landesverfassungsgericht. In W. Reutter (Ed.), *Landesverfassungsgerichte. Entwicklung—Aufbau—Funktionen* (pp. 371–388). Springer VS.

Gärditz, K. F. (2013). Landesverfassungsrichter. Zur personalen Dimension der Landesverfassungsgerichtsbarkeit. *Jahrbuch des öffentlichen Rechts der Gegenwart (N.F.), 61*, 449–493.

Glaab, M. (2017). Der Verfassungsgerichtshof Rheinland-Pfalz. In W. Reutter (Ed.), *Landesverfassungsgerichte. Entwicklung—Aufbau—Funktionen* (pp. 269–296). Springer VS.

Haack, S. (2010). Organisation und Arbeitsweise der Landesverfassungsgerichte in Deutschland. *Nordrhein-Westfälische Verwaltungsblätter, 24*(6), 216–221.

Häußler, R. (1994). *Der Konflikt zwischen Bundesverfassungsgericht und politischer Führung. Ein Beitrag zu Geschichte und Rechtsstellung des Bundesverfassungsgerichts*. Duncker & Humblot.

Heyde, W. (1983). Überblick über die Verfahren vor den Landesverfassungsgerichten mit Tabellen über die Häufigkeit der Verfahren (einschl. Schleswig-Holstein). In C. Starck & K. Stern (Eds.), *Landesverfassungsgerichtsbarkeit. Teilband II: Zuständigkeiten und Verfahren der Landesverfassungsgerichte* (pp. 1–16). Nomos.

Hildebrandt, A. (2020). Wen kümmert die Verschuldung? Landesverfassungsgerichte und Haushaltsrecht. In W. Reutter (Ed.), *Verfassungsgerichtsbarkeit in Bundesländern. Theoretische Perspektiven, methodische Überlegungen, empirische Befunde* (pp. 349–368). Springer VS.

Hofmann, J. (2018). Artikel 68 [Verfassungsgerichtshof]. In V. M. Haug (Ed.), *Verfassung des Landes Baden-Württemberg. Handkommentar* (pp. 1161–1251). Nomos.

Hoke, R. (1983). Verfassungsgerichtsbarkeit in den deutschen Ländern in der Tradition der deutschen Staatsgerichtsbarkeit. In C. Starck & K. Stern (Eds.), *Landesverfassungsgerichtsbarkeit. Teilband I: Geschichte, Organisation, Rechtsvergleichung* (pp. 25–102). Nomos.

Höreth, M. (2020). Der Beitrag der Landesverfassungsgerichte zur Unitarisierung des Bundesstaates. In W. Reutter (Ed.), *Verfassungsgerichtsbarkeit in Bundesländern. Theoretische Perspektiven, methodische Überlegungen und empirische Befunde* (pp. 49–76). Springer VS.

Hund, M. (2012). Würdigung der ausgeschiedenen Präsidentin und Richter. Einführung der neuen Präsidentin und Richter. In S. Schudoma (Ed.), *Zwanzig Jahre Berliner Verfassungsgerichtsbarkeit. Ansprachen anlässlich des Festaktes am 19. Juni 2012* (pp. 21–28). Carl Heymanns Verlag.

Kelsen, H. (2008). *Wer soll Hüter der Verfassung sein? Abhandlungen zur Theorie der Verfassungsgerichtsbarkeit in der pluralistischen, parlamentarischen Demokratie* [1930/31]. Edited by Robert Chr. van Ooyen. Mohr Siebeck.

Ketelhut, J. (2017). Der Verfassungsgerichtshof im Zwei-Städte-Staat. Der Staatsgerichtshof der Freien Hansestadt Bremen. In W. Reutter (Ed.), *Landesverfassungsgerichte. Entwicklung—Aufbau—Funktionen* (pp. 129–148). Springer VS.

Koch-Baumgarten, S. (2017). Der Staatsgerichtshof in Hessen zwischen unitarischem Bundesstaat, Mehrebenensystem und Landespolitik. In W. Reutter (Ed.), *Landesverfassungsgerichte. Entwicklung—Aufbau—Funktionen* (pp. 175–198). Springer VS.

Leibholz, G. (1957). Einleitung. *Jahrbuch des öffentlichen Rechts der Gegenwart (N.F.), 6*, 110–119.

Lembcke, O. W. (2015). Das Bundesverfassungsgericht und die Regierung Adenauer—vom Streit um den Status, zur Anerkennung der Autorität. In R. Chr. van Ooyen & M. H. W. Möllers

(Eds.), *Handbuch Bundesverfassungsgericht im politischen System* (pp. 231–244, 2nd ed.). Springer VS.

Lorenz, A. (2017). Das Verfassungsgericht des Landes Brandenburg als politisiertes Organ? Möglichkeiten und Grenzen politischer Einflussnahme. In W. Reutter (Ed.), *Landesverfassungsgerichte. Entwicklung—Aufbau—Funktionen* (pp. 105–128). Springer VS.

Meyer, P., & Hönnige, C. (2017). Der Niedersächsische Staatsgerichtshof. In W. Reutter (Ed.), *Landesverfassungsgerichte. Entwicklung—Aufbau—Funktionen* (pp. 219–242). Springer VS.

Niclauß, K. (2015). Der Parlamentarische Rat und das Bundesverfassungsgericht. In R. Chr. van Ooyen & M. H. W. Möllers (Eds.), *Handbuch Bundesverfassungsgericht im politischen System* (pp. 191–204, 2nd ed.). Springer VS.

Obrecht, M. (2017). Verfassungsgerichtshof Baden-Württemberg. In W. Reutter (Ed.), *Landesverfassungsgerichte. Entwicklung—Aufbau—Funktionen* (pp. 27–52). Springer VS.

Obrecht, M. (2020). Landesverfassungsgerichte, kommunale Selbstverwaltung und Gebietsreform. In W. Reutter (Ed.), *Verfassungsgerichtsbarkeit in Bundesländern. Theoretische Perspektiven, methodische Überlegungen und empirische Befunde* (pp. 323–348). Springer VS.

Papier, H.-J. (2018). "*Gesetz zur Änderung des Verfassungsgerichtshofgesetzes—Einführung der Individualverfassungsbeschwerde zum Verfassungsgerichtshof.*" Schriftliche Stellungnahme von Prof. Dr. Hans-Jürgen Papier. Landtag Nordrhein-Westfalen. Stellungnahme 17/615.

Patzelt, W. J. (2017). Der Verfassungsgerichtshof des Freistaates Sachsen. In W. Reutter (Ed.), *Landesverfassungsgerichte. Entwicklung—Aufbau—Funktionen* (pp. 323–346). Springer VS.

Pautsch, A. (2020). Landesverfassungsgerichte und direkte Demokratie. In W. Reutter (Ed.), *Verfassungsgerichtsbarkeit in Bundesländern. Theoretische Perspektiven, methodische Überlegungen und empirische Befunde* (pp. 323–348). Springer VS.

Pestalozza, H.-J. (1994). Das Landesverfassungsgericht von Sachsen-Anhalt. *LKV—Landes- und Kommunalverwaltung, 4*(1), 11–14.

Plöhn, J. (2020). Landesverfassungsgerichte und Landtagswahlen: Wahlrecht "ad libitum" oder unter "strict scrutiny"? In W. Reutter (Ed.), *Verfassungsgerichtsbarkeit in Bundesländern. Theoretische Perspektiven, methodische Überlegungen und empirische Befunde* (pp. 289–322). Springer VS.

Renzsch, W. (2020). "Steueroase" und "Abundanzumlage": die kommunale Finanzverfassung von Sachsen-Anhalt als Gegenstand der Landesverfassungsgerichtsbarkeit. In W. Reutter (Ed.), *Verfassungsgerichtsbarkeit in Bundesländern. Theoretische Perspektiven, methodische Überlegungen, empirische Befunde* (pp. 369–382). Springer VS.

Renzsch, W., & Schlüter, K. (2017). Das Landesverfassungsgericht von Sachsen-Anhalt. In W. Reutter (Ed.), *Landesverfassungsgerichte. Entwicklung—Aufbau—Funktionen* (pp. 347–370). Springer VS.

Reutter, W. (2017a). Landesverfassungsgerichte in der Bundesrepublik Deutschland. Eine Bestandsaufnahme. In W. Reutter (Ed.), *Landesverfassungsgerichte. Entwicklung—Aufbau—Funktionen* (pp. 1–26). Springer VS.

Reutter, W. (2017b). Der Verfassungsgerichtshof des Landes Berlin. In W. Reutter (Ed.), *Landesverfassungsgerichte. Entwicklung—Aufbau—Funktionen* (pp. 77–104). Springer VS.

Rütters, P. (2017). Saarland. Von der Verfassungskommission zum Verfassungsgerichtshof. In W. Reutter (Ed.), *Landesverfassungsgerichte. Entwicklung—Aufbau—Funktionen* (pp. 297–322). Springer VS.

Schiffers, R. (1984). "Ein mächtiger Pfeiler im Bau der Bundesrepublik". Das Gesetz über das Bundesverfassungsgericht vom 12. März 1951. *Vierteljahresheft für Zeitgeschichte, 32*(1), 66–102.

Schumann, E. (1983). Verfassungsbeschwerde (Grundrechtsklage) zu den Landesverfassungsgerichten. In C. Starck & K. Stern (Eds.), *Landesverfassungsgerichtsbarkeit. Teilband II: Zuständigkeiten und Verfahren der Landesverfassungsgerichte* (pp. 149–230). Nomos.

Starck, C. (1983). Der verfassungsrechtliche Status der Landesverfassungsgerichte. In C. Starck & K. Stern (Eds.), *Landesverfassungsgerichtsbarkeit. Teilband I: Geschichte, Organisation, Rechtsvergleichung* (pp. 155–182). Nomos.

courts are therefore "hybrid structures" between the "political sphere and the legal sphere" (Haack, 2010, p. 216). Elections of state constitutional justices, who fulfill their duties on a honorary and part-time basis, are thus inevitably political procedures. The political influence that manifests itself can be "channeled" and "moderated," but not eliminated (Haack, 2010, p. 216; Preuß, 1988; Reutter, 2018b; Gärditz, 2013).

6.1 Selection and Nomination of Justices

The election of a constitutional justice is a manifestation of two things: the beginning of a public office and the end of a political decision-making process. Both are preceded by a—partly pre-parliamentary—procedure. It is especially at this stage of the process that Landfried (2015, pp. 374–375), Will (2015, pp. 4–6), and others (Geuther & Remme, 2008) diagnose significant deficits in the Federal Republic of Germany's approach. Will finds the "practiced electoral procedures unsatisfactory in terms of their transparency" (Will, 2015, p. 5; see also Landfried, 2015, p. 374f.), and wants to design the "selection process of candidates for the election of judges" (Will, 2015, p. 5) in such a way that outsiders may understand it. In this context, she considers the formal "regulation of initiative rights for election proposals" "worth considering" (Will, 2015, p. 5), mentioning, among other things, Hesse as an example where parliamentary groups, the state government, and presidents of the highest state courts have the right to make proposals. In addition, Will recognizes a "different level of democratic legitimacy" (Will, 2015, p. 4) between "born" *(geborene)* and "elected" *(gekorene)* constitutional justices, i.e., between constitutional justices who achieve their posts *ex officio* and those who are elected by the state parliament. However, in the following I will show that Landfried and Will have based their recommendations partly on problematic assumptions, at least as far as the elections of constitutional justices in the states are concerned.

Eligibility and Selection of Constitutional Justices

Anyone who wants to become a constitutional justice must be eligible for election, that is, meet the criteria set out in the respective constitution or the constitutional court law (Gärditz, 2013, pp. 467–469; Reutter, 2017a, pp. 9–13; Harms-Ziegler, 1998). Of course, potential candidates are also checked to see whether they meet the requirements applicable in the respective state. In addition to aspects that relate to the composition of a court and which I will discuss later, four criteria can be distinguished in this context (Table 6.1).

Firstly—except in Baden-Württemberg—constitutional justices must be eligible to a German parliament, i.e., either to the Bundestag or to the respective state

Table 6.1 State Constitutional Justices: Number and Eligibility Criteria

	Number of justices	Deputies	Minimum age	Maximum age[a]	Eligibility for Parliament
BW	9	X	–	–/–	–
BAV	38	X	40	–/65	State Parliament
BER	9	–	35	–/–	Bundestag
BB	9	–	35	68/68	Bundestag
BRE	7	X	35	–/65	Bundestag
HAM	9	X	40	–/65	State Parliament
HES	11	X	35	–/65	State Parliament
MW	7	X	35	68/68	State Parliament
LS	9	X	35	–/–	State Parliament
NRW	7	X	35	–/65	State Parliament
RP	9	X	35	70/65	State Parliament
SLD	8th	X	35	–/–	State Parliament
SAY	9	X	35	70/65	Bundestag
SAT	7	X	40	–/–	State Parliament
SH	7	X	40	–/–	Bundestag
TH	9	X	35	70/65	State Parliament

[a] Legally defined maximum age for non-judicial members/legally defined maximum age for professional judges

Sources: self-conducted survey and compilation; state constitutions, constitutional court laws; Schmidt (2008, pp. 21)

parliament.[2] This excludes people who do not have German citizenship, who have been sentenced to at least one year in prison, who have been incapacitated, or who have been deprived of their right to vote by a court. Mecklenburg-Western Pomerania, Saxony, and Saxony-Anhalt also stipulate that anyone who "has violated the principles of humanity or the rule of law" or who has "worked for the former Ministry for State Security/Office for National Security of the German Democratic Party cannot become a constitutional justice" (§ 3 (4) Nos. 1 and 2 LVerfGG MW, also in: § 2 (4) Nos. 1 and 2 SächsVerfGHG; similar: § 6 (1) Nos. 1 and 2 SachsAnhVerfGG).[3]

Secondly, eligibility for election to the Bundestag—as in Berlin (§ 3 (1) BerlVerfGHG)—expands the choice and increases the "legal distance from the [...] often closely interwoven 'legal scene' in an office-appropriate manner" (Gärditz, 2013, p. 468). The clause promises that only those who can be elected to the respective state parliament, have ties to their homeland, and have greater knowledge of the state can become a constitutional justice. In total, constitutional justices must be eligible for election to the Bundestag in five states and to the state parliament in ten

[2] In principle, constitutional justices may not simultaneously be members of the state parliament. In Bavaria, however, this incompatibility has only been in effect since 1991; before that, members of the state parliament were repeatedly elected as constitutional judges.

[3] This can also be grounds for impeachment, as I will discuss below.

office" and whether the additional burden is the reason why a candidate was persuaded to take this office with the reassurance that he had only to sign rulings (Diwell, 2012, p. 31). Recruitment problems also arose at the Thuringian Constitutional Court in 1994/95 because the first election's conditions stipulated that constitutional justices should reside in Thuringia. Accordingly, the "attraction of suitable judges for the office of constitutional justice [...] had proven to be extremely difficult" (Landtag TH, LT-Drs. 2/106 of January 24, 1995, p. 1). The Thuringian Constitutional Court's first nine constitutional justices and their deputies were only found, proposed, and elected after the Constitutional Court Law's residency clause was deleted (Reutter, 2019d).

On the other hand, it should be noted that the selection of judges for constitutional courts is based on non-transparent procedures in which proportional aspects also play a role. This mode is repeated in the act of parliamentary creation, to which I will return later, because elections are usually carried out secretly and without debate. However, it is doubtful whether the greater transparency demanded by Rosemarie Will in such selection procedures would contribute to stronger judicial legitimacy: The possibility of the right to initiate the procedure, which she described as "worth considering," exists in a whole series of states. In addition, Will remains unclear as to how a selection process should be organized in a publicly understandable way. Finally, a balance must be struck between the requirement of transparency arising from democratic theory and the efficient fulfillment of a parliamentary task.

Who Has the Privilege to Propose Candidates and Who Proposes Candidates?

According to Sascha Kneip (2008, p. 640), only those EU member states that give the opposition an institutionalized say in the selection of justices come close to the "ideal of a neutral and independent constitutional court." Judicial independence is only guaranteed where a "supermajority" is required for the parliamentary election of a constitutional justice (see also Kneip, 2020). Yet application of this standard would mean constitutional jurisprudence in the German states has a problem.

The right to propose a justice for election to a state parliament is by no means based solely on constitutional provisions in the states. Only three state constitutions contain provisions on the right to make proposals (Art. 65 (2) HmbVerf; Art. 52 (3) Verf MW; Art. 134 (4) RhPfVerf; Blumenthal, 2017, pp. 151–155; Glaab, 2017, pp. 274–279; Ewert & Hein, 2017, pp. 201–205). And in no state is the right to submit proposals to parliament for the election of constitutional justices conclusively standardized in the basic legal order. Yet some constitutional court laws are also silent in this regard: Only 11 states have corresponding regulations, and these can be changed with a simple majority. In 12 states, the provisions of the state parliaments' rules of procedure apply either alone or as a supplement to the Constitutional Court Law.

It follows from these stipulations that those empowered to propose candidates for the state constitutional court to the respective state parliament can include the following: the state government (in six states), parliamentary groups (twelve states), individual members of parliament (five), a parliamentary committee (six), presidiums or councils of elders (four), and representatives of the highest state courts (three) (Table 6.2).

Only in a minority of states are the constitutional justices elected with a two-thirds majority of the legal members; in five others, a "supermajority" of cast votes is required. Three states deem a governmental majority sufficient; Baden-Württemberg accepts a relative majority, Bavaria and Bremen even a simple one (Obrecht 2017, pp. 30-33; Weigl 2017, pp. 56-62; Ketelhut 2017, pp. 137–138). Hesse makes a distinction between the professional judges, who are elected by the electoral committee with a two-thirds majority, and the other members, for whom a simple majority in the plenary is sufficient (Koch-Baumgarten, 2017, pp. 183–185). In Hamburg, the constitutional court justices can also be elected with a simple majority, without—as in Bavaria and Baden-Württemberg—any "form of minority protection" being provided for through additional procedural regulations (Wittreck, 2006, p. 503).

Overall, this results in a heterogeneous picture of legal standardization: Nomination rights and procedures not only arise from legal sources that differ in the hierarchy of norms, but they also assign the privilege of suggesting candidates for the election of constitutional justices to different entities. Representatives of the executive branch can be found here as well as representatives of the legislative or judicial branches. In addition, only in exceptional cases were candidates nominated without a majority. In the nine states listed in Table 6.3, 1319 candidates were nominated in a total of 74 electoral periods, of which 1180, i.e., around 90%, received the required majority. In three states (MW, SAT, SH), all proposed candidates were elected.[4]

These findings support the assumption that elections of constitutional justices generally follow consensual decision-making patterns. Marcus Obrecht (2017, p. 32) reports that the judicial elections in Baden-Württemberg were based on inter-party proposals that generally met with broad approval—a surprising harmony, given that this state only requires a relative majority of votes. Agreements between parliamentary parties are not required. However, minority parliamentary parties are also given the opportunity to propose candidates for election to the constitutional court. That is why, in 2018, Baden-Württemberg's AfD was able to nominate a candidate, who received more "yes" than "no" votes in the second round of voting and thus reached the required majority (Landtag BW, PlPr. 16/63 from June 6th, 2018, p. 3764 and 16/65 from June 14th, 2018, p. 3890). In contrast, in 1997 and 2000, the Greens failed to have "their" candidates elected to what was then the State Court of Justice (Hofmann, 2018, p. 1245f. [fn 689]).

[4]Of the nominated candidates, 10 were not elected in Baden-Württemberg, 35 in Bavaria, 8 in Brandenburg, 2 each in Berlin and Saxony, and 15 in Thuringia. In addition, there are 52 separate elections for presidents and vice-presidents in Baden-Württemberg, Bavaria, and Berlin.

6.2 Election of Justices

The dominant idea in the states is that constitutional justices should be elected by a parliament. While other appointment procedures (such as ex-officio membership) exist,[5] they conflict with the democratic requirements that arise from the constitutional courts' quality (Will, 2015, p. 4f.). "Elected" and "born" members of constitutional courts are based on different chains of legitimacy: The former are elected by the state parliament, the latter are appointed by the minister (Gärditz, 2013, p. 463). In 2015, North Rhine-Westphalia abolished ex officio membership in order to level out "status differences" between "born" and "elected" members (Thierse & Hohl, 2017, p. 245). However, I am devoting this part of my study exclusively to the election of constitutional justices by state parliaments.

In almost all states, constitutional justices are elected by the general assembly of the members of parliament, the plenary. Hesse alone assigns the task to elect professional judges to the State Constitutional Court to an election committee (§ 5 (2) HessStGHG; Koch-Baumgarten, 2017, pp. 183–185). These elections usually take place "secretly" and always "without discussion." It is assumed that the election has a "real decision-making function, not just a confirmation function" (Platter, 2008, p. 16). As mentioned, in the eight states listed in Table 6.3, around one in ten proposals failed to achieve the necessary majority. In some state parliaments, candidates are scheduled to be heard in committees. In others, such hearings take place informally and in still others, candidates present themselves in parliamentary groups. From the perspective of democratic theory, this certainly merits criticism: The parliamentary transparency requirement is being reduced to a minimum. Yet a possible justification lies in the fact that limited publicity in the election process of constitutional justices serves to fulfill the parliamentary creative function.

The determination of majority requirements and the design of the parliamentary election procedures are intended to prevent party politicization of the constitutional courts and to ensure that elections of constitutional justices are carried out according to democratic principles. There is a widespread expectation that constitutional justices will be elected with a "supermajority." Only support from across the aisles can sustain the justices' independence, maintain the court's neutrality, and integrate effectively the opposition into this process (Kneip, 2008, p. 639 f., Hönnige, 2007, p. 108f., Steinsdorff, 2009, p. 209; Gärditz, 2013, pp. 460f.; Bettermann, 1981). As explained, a simple, relative, or absolute majority is sufficient in four states; in addition, in Hesse the six "remaining members"

[5] This still exists at the Bremen State Court of Justice and at the Rhineland-Palatinate Constitutional Court, and it existed in North Rhine-Westphalia until 2017, in Saarland until 1979, and in Hamburg until 1996; in Bavaria, a president of the three higher regional courts belongs to the Constitutional Court. This is intended to guarantee "predictability and stability of the application of the law" (Gärditz, 2013, p. 461).

of the State Court of Justice are elected with a simple majority.[6] These relatively low majority quotas have faced repeated criticism (Gärditz, 2013, pp. 477f.; Bettermann, 1981). Bavaria has made several attempts to change the majority requirement.

However, three points are worth mentioning in this context. First, the legal majority requirement only allows partial statements to be made about whether the parliamentary minority influences the court's composition. In Bavaria, judges are nominated and elected according to the principle of proportional representation. This grants minority parties with the right to make proposals based on their share in the state parliament. In addition, in the constitutional courts of Baden-Württemberg, Bavaria, and, if one follows press reports, Mecklenburg-Western Pomerania, we find justices who were proposed by the AfD and were elected by the respective state parliament (Landtag BW, PlPr. 16/21 of December 14th, 2016, p. 1031 and 16/65 of June 14th, 2018, p. 3890ff.; Landtag BAV, PlPr. 18/5 of December 11th, 2018, pp. 193 and 205; Hein, 2018; Reutter, 2019a). In Brandenburg, Bremen, and Berlin, the parliamentary groups or "political forces" are granted the right to make proposals, which, as far as I can verify, is reflected in the constitutional courts' compositions (Reutter, 2017b, 2018a, 2018b). Secondly, the requirement for a "supermajority" increases the need for consensus and thus the need for informal agreements (Platter, 2008, p. 15).[7] Finally, I should mention that the support that constitutional justices receive in parliamentary elections overwhelmingly surpasses the additional requirement. In the eight states listed in Table 6.4, on average almost nine out of ten MPs who cast a vote and more that 80% of all MPs voted on average for the eventually elected constitutional justices. The approval was therefore generally well above the required majority. These findings confirm Gärditz's (2013, p. 465) assumption that a "one-sided politicization" of constitutional courts by the respective parliamentary majority did not take place.

[6] According to Article 69 (2) and (3) BayVerf in conjunction with Section 4 BayVerfGHG, constitutional judges are to be elected "by the state parliament." No specifically defined majority is required. This means that Section 44 GO BAV LT applies, according to which the person who receives more than half of the valid votes cast is elected.

[7] Such criticism is often simply an expression of fundamental party prudery. Bettermann's (1981) analysis is an eloquent example. He vehemently advocates for a qualified majority requirement in order to give the parliamentary minority "greater influence on the composition of the constitutional courts" (Bettermann, 1981, p. 744). At the same time, however, he warns against "compensation deals," "cronyism," and "political immorality," which he associates with party democracy and denounces in a blanket manner (Bettermann, 1981, p. 746).

sion in the event of inadmissible or obviously unfounded constitutional complaints (Obrecht, 2017, p. 35). It is noticeable that—apart from Saarland (Rütters, 2017)—all states have an odd number of constitutional justices. Since abstentions are not possible and motions are considered rejected in the event of a tie, this provides a mathematical guarantee of clear majorities.

(b) According to Ernst-Wolfgang Böckenförde, one criterion is particularly important for the composition of a constitutional court: a "high [legal] qualification" of the justices (Böckenförde, 1999, p. 177; similar: BVerfG, decision of July 23rd, 1998, 1 BvR 2470/94, Rn. 35; Sanders & Danwitz 2018, p. 807; Bettermann, 1981, p. 723f.). The state constitution makers and state legislators saw this differently or at least qualified the criterion: They not only set maximum and minimum ages, but also quotas for women and men or for professional and lay judges (Table 6.5). In five states, at least three constitutional justices must or should be men and three women; in two others, gender "should" be adequately taken into account (Reutter, 2017b, pp. 85–87; Lorenz, 2017, pp. 110–117; Meyer & Hönnige, 2017, pp. 223f.; Glaab, 2017, p. 276; Rütters, 2017, pp. 303–306).

These requirements are supplemented by provisions on the composition of the courts (Table 6.5). All state constitutional courts have a minimum number of professional judges; some must, others may, have lay judges; three (BAV, SH, and NRW [since 2017]) bar lay judges from participating. From a legal perspective, lay judges could even form the majority in five state constitutional courts (BRE, HES, NRW, RP, SLD).[9] Rosemarie Will (2015, p. 6), former constitutional justice in Brandenburg, assesses the "cooperation experienced with the legal lay-people in the [Brandenburg State Constitutional Court] as entirely positive." For Klaus Ferdinand Gärditz (2013, p. 473), however, "the balance sheet is sobering" (Gärditz, 2013, p. 473): He claims that only a few lay judges were appointed, and these proved meaningless in the courts' practice (p. 473f.; see also Rinken, 2000, p. 95).

If one examines the constitutional courts' compositions based on the legal dimensions, some special features emerge (Table 6.6):

- On average, around 15% of elected constitutional justices are female, with the shares varying between around 11 and 40%. These variations are far from coincidental: Female justices are most strongly represented where appropriate legal quotas exist; the proportion is lowest in Bavaria. It should also be noted that the information refers to different time periods. Gärditz (2013, p. 487) reports that in 2012, female justices at the state court of justice level made up a majority only in Bremen.
- With the exception of the Constitutional Court of Baden-Württemberg—which mandates a third parity of professional judges, judges qualified to hold judicial office, and lay judges—professional judges make up the largest group in all state

[9] I have no scope here to discuss the reasons for the inclusion of lay judges in constitutional courts; see Fiedler (1983, p. 128–133); Bachof (1968, p. 4), Gärditz (2013, p. 475f.), Chap. 4.

Table 6.5 Composition of the State Constitutional Courts: Legal Requirements (Without Deputies; as of December 31st, 2018)

	Number of statutory justices	Ex-officio justices	Professional judges	"Other Justices"[a]	Lay justices[b]	Minimum number of female Judges[c]
BW	9	–	3	3	3	0
BAV	38	–	23	15[d]	0	0
BER	9	–	3	6	(3)	3
BB	9	–	3	6	(3)	(3)
BRE	7	1	3	4	(4)	0
HAM	9	–	4	5	(3)	0
HES	11	–	5	6	(6)	0
MW	7	–	2	5	(3)	0
LS	9	–	3[e]	6	(3)	(3)
NRW	7	–	3	4	0	0
RP	9	1	4	5	(5)	0
SLD[f]	8	–	2	6	0	(3)
SAY	9	–	5	4	(4)	0
SAT	7	–	3	4	(4)	(3)
SH	7	–	3	4	0	0
TH	9	–	3	6	(3)	0

[a] Members of the constitutional court with or without qualifications for judicial office (excluding professional judges)
[b] Number of lay judges—in brackets the number of judges who may, but do not have to, be qualified to hold judicial office
[c] Number of female justices—in brackets the number of female justices who "should" be members of the constitutional court
[d] In Bavaria, the non-professional judge members "should" have the qualifications to hold judicial office (§ 5 (1) BayVerfGHG)
[e] In Lower Saxony, three of the members "should" be professional judges (§ 1 (2) NdsStGHG)
[f] In Saarland, justices must have the qualification to hold judicial office or to "higher administrative service: "At least two members [...] should be professional judges and belong to a higher regional court" (§ 2 (2) SaarlVerfGHG)
Sources: self-compiled; state constitutions and constitutional court laws

constitutional courts. In Bavaria, Mecklenburg-Western Pomerania, Saxony, and Schleswig-Holstein their share is well over 50%. In addition, professional judges usually also provide the president and/or vice president. This supports the assumption that professional judges in the states also shape constitutional jurisprudence. In addition to Baden-Württemberg, professional judges are comparatively poorly represented in Thuringia (Obrecht, 2017, pp. 30–35; Lembcke, 2017, pp. 393–396). The Bavarian Constitutional Court has a "special feature" in that the "most important proceedings" are decided exclusively by professional judges (Gärditz, 2013, p. 477). In combination with the majority requirement and the possibility of re-election of constitutional justices, this results in a problematic dependence on, or at least proximity to, the government majority. Gärditz (2013, p. 477) therefore rightly doubts whether the "extensive and exclusive

According to Klaus Ferdinand Gärditz (2013, p. 492f.), the judicial composition of state constitutional courts shows systematic "deficits." Gärditz argues that a "pluralistically structured state" must also have a sociologically pluralistic judgeship in the state constitutional courts as a "key element." However, the state constitutional courts have a "one-sided" professional judicial identity that precludes turning them into alternative "personnel law models of institutionalized constitutional jurisdiction" (Gärditz, 2013, p. 493). My findings only partially confirm this conclusion: The state constitutional courts included only a few lay judges and professors of law, that is, in some courts they were not represented at all. Likewise, women have remained a minority in many such courts, and lawyers are by no means found in relevant numbers in all of them. In overview, however, the composition of the constitutional courts in the states creates a markedly plural picture. Insofar they complement and complete the Federal Constitutional Court's demographic structure.

The composition of the courts can therefore also be discussed from a different perspective. The elections of constitutional justices and their court's makeup are subject to different normative requirements. While the appointment or election of justices follows the imperative of input legitimacy, i.e., is based on an uninterrupted chain of legitimacy that must find its starting point in the sovereign, the question of composition is aimed at the output of these processes, i.e., whether the state constitutional court's composition meets democratic and constitutional requirements (Reutter, 2022, pp.100–105; Reutter, 2020, pp. 218–224). From a constitutional perspective, the focus is on "high qualifications of judges and the judicial nature of their administration" (Böckenförde, 1999: 177). In this view, a constitutional court should be composed of legal experts who are experienced in constitutional law and who are qualified to serve as justices, specifically: professional judges, lawyers, and professors of law. Accordingly, lay judges are neither necessary nor desirable. In addition, considerations about the social, ethnic, or gender "representativeness" of constitutional courts should remain irrelevant. If, on the other hand, one considers constitutional courts in the tradition of Smend as a socio-political integration authority—or as an "integration factor and as a medium for creating identity" (Papier, 2020, p. 38)—representativeness must be taken into account. From this perspective, a heterogeneous composition based on profession, gender, age, social background, or political orientation is a productive prerequisite for the quality of judicial deliberation and for the social acceptance of decisions.

In his study, Uwe Kranenpohl (2010) found that the Federal Constitutional Court's plural composition counteracts a tendency towards conformity that is counterproductive to judicial decision-making. This plural composition ensures that deliberations tend to be discourse-oriented and open-ended. All of the justices Kranenpohl interviewed were of the opinion that the Federal Constitutional Court's composition had "clear advantages" compared to that of constitutional courts consisting solely of professional judges (Kranenpohl, 2010, p. 231). The diverging forms of legal application and interpretation by professional judges, lawyers, and law professors complemented each other productively.

However, no studies have so far shown whether and to what extent the composition of state constitutional courts influences judicial decision-making (see however

Chap. 7). I can thus only examine whether and to what extent state constitutional courts support the imperative of diversity, which is central to the network of constitutional courts, and follow the principle of pluralism. I have checked this along three dimensions: composition by gender, by main occupation, and by age. I have (a) described the extent of gender parity with the percentage of female justices, (b) determined professional heterogeneity using the fractionalization index (F), which is commonly used in diversity research, and (c) recorded the variance in the judges' age composition using the coefficient of variation (KOV) (Table 6.7).

(a) State constitutional courts were "male bastions" until the 1990s (Fig. 6.1). Until 1973, only the Bavarian Constitutional Court and the Hessian State Court of Justice had ever had female justices. A (very) slight improvement occurred in the 1980s, when the proportion of female justices increased to 6.4%, almost doubling the figures of the previous decade. It was not until this period that the share of female justices elected to the German state constitutional courts began to increase at a consistent rate. Statistically aggregated, this means that almost

Table 6.7 Diversity in State Constitutional Courts: Share of Female Judges (Percent), Professional Fractionalization (F), and Variance in Age Spectrums (KOV)

	Share of female justices[a] (in %)	Professional fractionalization[b] (F)	Variance of age spectra[c] (KOV)
BW	11.8	0.70	0.14
BAV	11.2	0.60	0.14
B.B	39.0	0.71	0.14
BER	40.5	0.61	0.15
BRE	33.3	0.62	0.23
HAM	24.1	0.48	0.16
HES	15.2	0.68	0.15
MW	16.7	0.51	0.15
NO	17.3	0.59	0.11
NRW	13.0	0.52	0.14
SLD	10.4	0.69	n/a
RP	11.0	0.65	0.14
SAY	21.7	0.55	0.13
SAT	29.4	0.66	0.14
SH	28.6	0.36	0.15
Th	23.8	0.70	0.12
Ø	16.5	0.64	0.14

[a] Where applicable, including deputies (except for Bavaria)
[b] Without deputies—the fractionalization index "F" can take values between 0 (absolute homogeneity) and 1 (absolute heterogeneity) and is calculated by subtracting the sum of the squared proportions of a group in a population from the value 1; see Schaeffer (2016, pp. 49 and 54f)
[c] Including deputies (without Bavaria)—KOV = s/x, where; s = standard deviation, x = mean; empirical basis: 2223 voting processes; the higher KOV, the larger the average age range; see Quatember (2008, p. 55)
Sources: self-conducted surveys and calculations

ences between the courts are also notable, as their fractionalizations fluctuate between 0.4 (SH) and 0.7 (BW, TH). In summary, my findings allow three conclusions: State constitutional courts are professionally pluralistic in composition; the professional composition changes over time; and the element that characterizes state constitutional jurisprudence, namely the lay judges, has continuously lost importance.

(c) As with the other two dimensions, some states also legally regulate the age of judges. While setting a maximum age is intended to ensure fitness for service, a specified minimum age is linked to sufficient life experience. What is of particular interest for the present context is how large the age variance is that is represented in a court. This can be determined using the coefficient of variation (KOV), which includes two measures: the average age when taking office and the standard deviation. Not surprisingly, the KOV only shows a small spread. If one ignores the outlier Bremen, the coefficient of variation only fluctuates marginally between 0.12 and 0.15. Age-wise, constitutional courts are a rather homogeneous group. Only the Brandenburg Constitutional Court's justices were, on average, younger than 50 when they took office (Reutter 2018c), while the average age in all other courts was between 50 and almost 58 years.

With Stefan Haack (2010, p. 218) and in contrast to Klaus Ferdinand Gärditz (2013, p. 492), I can therefore summarize that the regulations on the election mode, the electoral procedures carried out, as well as the modes for ending a judicial office serve to "channel" and "moderate" the political influence of parties. At the same time, they keep this influence "recognizable". The "dual nature" (Haack, 2010, p. 218) of the state constitutional courts also corresponds to their composition: While "legally trained judges" mark state constitutional courts as judicial bodies in which an "effective form of judicial work can be practiced," (Haack, 2010, p. 218) the inclusion of non-judicial groups, or even non-lawyers, supports the integration function of these constitutional bodies. In this way, the state constitutional courts make their own contribution to the personal dimension in the network of German constitutional courts. In this respect, the constitutional court network is not just a federal structure—rather, it reproduces and underpins the fundamental principles of federalism of diversity and openness.

6.4 End of Office, Length of Term, Re-election, and Removal from Office

As with the selection, parliamentary election, and composition of the state constitutional justices, the end of office and term of office are also characterized by the dual character of the state constitutional courts as constitutional bodies and as courts. The idea that constitutional jurisprudence (like all jurisprudence) requires continuity, judicial experience, and stability arises more from the nature of the court. Such ideas are promoted by fixed terms of office, the possibility of re-election, and the fact that constitutional justices cannot be removed from office, or only with difficulty. At the same time, constitutional bodies must be legitimized democratically, and should be able to manifest both social change and divergent constitutional views. Judicial continuity and judicial stability must not mutate into "petrification" any more than the judiciary's continuous renewal and "regular refreshment" (Gärditz, 2013, p. 464) must call into question the constitutional courts' independence. Within this spectrum, the states' legal standards and political practices diverge and vary significantly in regards to (a) term of office, (b) the possibility of re-election, and (c) removal from office (Table 6.9):

(a) Term of office: No state appoints justices at constitutional courts for life. Only in the two states in which justices are ex officio members of the constitutional court is permanent exercise of office possible—although still not for life. Those states that come closest to the democratic imperative are those in which all constitutional court justices are elected in each legislative period. In its pure form, this is true only of Bremen; in Bavaria and Hesse, at least some of the judges' judicial office is tied to the parliamentary term. For the remaining judges, the statutory term of office is between 6 and 12 years, with an average of 7.8 years.
(b) Re-election: Apparently independent of the term of office, the states determined whether justices can be re-elected (Table 6.9). Berlin, Mecklenburg-Western Pomerania, and Brandenburg all rule out re-election. Oddly enough, although in Berlin the term of office is legally limited to 7 years, in fact the justices serve on average 7.8 years at the Constitutional Court. Brandenburg's lies at 10 years, and Mecklenburg-Western Pomerania's 12 years trumps all other states. Six states, all with terms of office of either 6 or 7 years, allow justices to be re-elected once. In the remaining states, where justices can be re-elected indefinitely, the term of office varies between 6 and 9 years. If re-election is possible, the effective term of office is always significantly longer than that required by law; in individual cases it was even almost 30 years. Scholars usually view the possibility of re-election critically. According to Sven Leunig (2023, p. 211), it could provoke "an opportunistic orientation towards the political majority." Martina Flick (2011, p. 50) argues that there is a decidedly "political component" where the term of office of constitutional justices is linked to the legislative period (Bavaria, Bremen, Hesse) and re-election is possible (Harms-Ziegler, 1998, p. 199). Such assumptions are difficult to prove. Gärditz, e.g., (2013, p. 465) doubts such a causal link. So far, there have been "no recognizable conflicts" when constitutional justices had been re-elected. Gärditz explains this with the fact that honorary constitutional justices are not materially and economically dependent on their office; the power to decide on the continuation of their office is therefore hardly an instrument for influencing justices (Gärditz, 2013, p. 465; Wittreck, 2006, p. 507).

reserves of context-sensitive dogma formation" (Gärditz, 2013, p. 493). I cannot draw such far-reaching and emphatic conclusions on the basis of my preceding analysis, with which I examined only selection, election, the courts' composition, and end of office. I have not examined whether and to what extent this has consequences for decision-making, or for adjudication practice in general. After all, I identified quite considerable differences between the states: All examined dimensions—selection, parliamentary elections, the composition as well as the end of office and term of office—exhibited varying possible combinations and characteristics that cannot be condensed into models or consistent ideal types. The only thing they have in common is that the parliamentary election of justices is the central legitimation mechanism. At the same time, it can be said that the state parliaments were able to effectively fulfill their task in this area. Although individual candidates occasionally failed, or a second round of voting was required, this only confirms the nature of the parliamentary decision—namely, to not only confirm proposals, but to provide the candidates with broad legitimacy. It would be both naive and normatively undesirable to argue that procedures for electing or appointing constitutional justices in democracies could, or should, be immunized against political influences. Rather, it is important to make an "objective closeness to politics compatible with a constitutionally required independence from political forces" (Haack, 2010, p. 217). The regulations for the election of constitutional justices can "only serve to channel, moderate and make this influence recognizable" (Haack, 2010, p. 218). The elections and voting procedures examined here meet this requirement.

There is no evidence of one-sided party politicization of constitutional justice elections. This applies both to parliamentary elections and to influencing incumbent justices. Elections of state constitutional justices are exclusive acts of parliaments in which party committees play no empirically conspicuous role and which also evade simple majority dominance. The electoral procedures are based on consensus democracy and are designed to be minority-friendly even where agreements across the aisle are not necessary. The majority requirement in the states is apparently less important than is often assumed. Parliamentary parties in opposition can also influence the election of constitutional justices and the courts' composition through other procedural requirements. Jes Möller, President of the Brandenburg State Constitutional Court, confirms that there has been no "attempt to influence the Constitutional Court yet"; not even "a trace of an attempt to do so" has appeared (Landtag BB, P-RA 5/42 of August 22nd, 2013, p. 13f.). However, the practice in Bavaria and Saxony seems to be problematic. In these states, the state governments and the parliamentary majority have gained influence that certainly gives rise to criticism. Rights of nomination, the possibility of unlimited re-election, and the large proportion of professional judges privilege the executive branch in these states, even if the final election is formally held by the state parliaments.

According to Gärditz (2013, p. 493), the judiciary's composition shows "clear deficits." The state constitutional courts' ruling practice is often characterized by professional judges, and "in terms of personnel" they are "rather small copies of the Federal Constitutional Court" (Gärditz, 2013, p. 485). Practically no use is made of the opportunity to "pluralize the bench in professional and social terms," a criticism that particularly applies the positions reserved for "non-lawyers," which have often been filled by "full lawyers of different backgrounds" (Gärditz, 2013, p. 486). My findings and analysis can only partially confirm this conclusion. The courts' compositions show a considerable range of variations and at least selectively complement the (sociologically) legal monopoly at the Federal Constitutional Court.

References

Bachof, O. (1968). Der Staatsgerichtshof für das Land Baden-Württemberg. In *Rechtswissenschaftliche Abteilung der Rechts- und Wirtschaftswissenschaftlichen Fakultät der Universität Tübingen, Tübinger Festschrift für Eduard Kern* (pp. 1–19). J.C.B. Mohr.

Bettermann, K. A. (1981). Opposition und Verfassungsrichterwahl. In H. Bernstein, U. Drobnig, & H. Kötz (Eds.), *Festschrift für Konrad Zweigert zum 70. Geburtstag* (pp. 723–746). J.C.B. Mohr.

Blumenthal, J. V. (2017). Das Hamburgische Verfassungsgericht. Schiedsrichter zwischen Senat, Bürgerschaft und Volk. In W. Reutter (Ed.), *Landesverfassungsgerichte. Entwicklung—Aufbau—Funktionen* (pp. 149–175). Springer VS.

Böckenförde, E.-W. (1999). Verfassungsgerichtsbarkeit. Strukturfragen, Organisation, Legitimation. In E.-W. Böckenförde (Ed.), *Staat, Nation, Europa. Studien zur Verfassungslehre, Verfassungstheorie und Rechtsphilosophie* (pp. 157–182). Suhrkamp.

Bryde, B.-O. (1998). Die Verfassungsgerichtsbarkeit in der Rechtssoziologie. In J. Brand & D. Strempel (Eds.), *Soziologie des Rechts. Festschrift für Erhard Blankenburg zum 60. Geburtstag* (pp. 491–504). Nomos.

Bryde, B.-O. (2000). Juristensoziologie. In H. Dreier (Ed.), *Rechtssoziologie am Ende des 20. Jahrhunderts* (pp. 137–155). Mohr Siebeck.

Deutscher Richterbund (Ed.). (1993ff.). *Handbuch der Justiz: Die Träger und Organe der rechtsprechenden Gewalt in der Bundesrepublik Deutschland*. C.F. Müller.

Diwell, M. (2012). Geburtstagswünsche. In S. Schudoma (Ed.), *Zwanzig Jahre Berliner Verfassungsgerichtsbarkeit. Ansprachen anlässlich des Festaktes am 19. Juni 2012* (pp. 29–34). Carl Heymanns Verlag.

Ewert, S., & Hein, M. (2017). Das Landesverfassungsgericht Mecklenburg-Vorpommern. In W. Reutter (Ed.), *Landesverfassungsgerichte. Entwicklung—Aufbau—Funktionen* (pp. 199–218). Springer VS.

Fiedler, W. (1983). Die Entstehung der Landesverfassungsgerichtsbarkeit nach dem Zweiten Weltkrieg. In C. Starck & K. Stern (Eds.), *Landesverfassungsgerichtsbarkeit. Teilband I: Geschichte, Organisation, Rechtsvergleichung* (pp. 103–154). Nomos.

Flick, M. (2011). *Organstreitverfahren vor den Landesverfassungsgerichten. Eine politikwissenschaftliche Untersuchung*. Peter Lang.

Flick Witzig, M. (2017). Das Schleswig-Holsteinische Landesverfassungsgericht. In W. Reutter (Ed.), *Landesverfassungsgerichte. Entwicklung—Aufbau—Funktionen* (pp. 371–388). Springer VS.

Gärditz, K. F. (2013). Landesverfassungsrichter. Zur personalen Dimension der Landesverfassungsgerichtsbarkeit. *Jahrbuch des öffentlichen Rechts der Gegenwart (N.F.), 61*, 449–493.

Geuther, G., & Remme, K. (2008). Undemokratischer als die Papstwahl? *Die Ernennung der Richter am Bundesverfassungsgericht*. Retrieved from https://www.deutschlandfunk.de/undemokratischer-als-die-papstwahl.724.de.html?dram:article_id=99030

Glaab, M. (2017). Der Verfassungsgerichtshof Rheinland-Pfalz. In W. Reutter (Ed.), *Landesverfassungsgerichte. Entwicklung—Aufbau—Funktionen* (pp. 269–296). Springer VS.

Haack, S. (2010). Organisation und Arbeitsweise der Landesverfassungsgerichte in Deutschland. *Nordrhein-Westfälische Verwaltungsblätter, 24*(6), 216–221.

Table 7.1 Strength of Judicial Decisions: Components and Elements (according to Pócza et al., 2017: 1564)

Ruling	Rejection or refusal (0.0)	Unconstitutionality by legislative omission (0.25)	Procedural unconstitutionality (1.0)	Constitutional requirements (2.0)	Substantive unconstitutionality (5.0)	Constitutional interpretation in abstracto (7.0)
Completeness	Qualitative partial annulment (0.0)	Quantitative partial annulment (1.0)		Complete annulment (2.0)		
Timing	Pro futuro (0.0)	Ex nunc (0.5)		Ex tunc (1.0)		
Prescription	No prescription (0.0)	Non-binding prescription (1.0)		Directive/binding prescription (2.0)		

Source: According to Pócza et al. (2017, p. 1564)

judgments and decisions such courts made during this period, their publication by the respective constitutional court qualified them all as relevant. For the Bavarian Constitutional Court, which is not represented in the collection, I took into account all 104 decisions the court has published online since 1997. For the State Court of Justice of North Rhine-Westphalia, I selected 70 decisions about which press releases have been issued since 1994. For the Rhineland-Palatinate Constitutional Court, I included all 23 decisions published online since 2010. In total, my data corpus consists of 1172 decisions.

If one examines the constitutional jurisprudence in the states on this basis, two findings emerge (Table 7.2). Firstly, the widely expressed assumption that constitutional courts have an inherent tendency towards judicialization (Landfried, 1984; Hirschl, 2007; Stone Sweet, 2000) is not confirmed in the German states. On the contrary, the number of judgments that qualify as "strong" in the defined sense amount to just two. In the states, the state constitutional courts' task is limited to controlling state actions against the standards of the state constitution. They were unable to distinguish themselves as a law-making authority, regardless of the differences between the states. The State Constitutional Court of Saxony-Anhalt made 21 decisions that were of medium strength, followed by the Thuringian Constitutional Court's 15 (of 74). Measured by the arithmetic mean, the State Court of Justice of Lower Saxony makes the strongest decisions (1.81), followed by the Constitutional Court of Saxony-Anhalt (1.70) and the Thuringian Constitutional Court (1.65). The Berlin Constitutional Court (0.18) and the Brandenburg State Constitutional Court

Table 7.2 Strength of Decisions of Constitutional Courts in German States

Land	No. of all decisions	Number of decisions with …			Mean
		0–4 pts.	4.5–8 pts.	8.5–12 pts.	
BW	30	26	4	0	0.93
BAV	147	129	17	1	0.88
BER	237	231	6	0	0.18
BB	195	182	13	0	0.49
BRE	27	22	5	0	1.13
HAM	34	29	4	1	1.00
HES	71	66	5	0	0.54
MW	50	40	10	0	1.23
NO	18	13	5	0	1.81
NRW	81	70	11	0	0.99
RP	30	26	4	0	0.98
SLD	19	17	2	0	0.58
SAY	78	68	10	0	0.99
SAT	79	58	21	0	1.70
SH	12	9	3	0	1.46
TH	64	49	15	0	1.65
Σ	1172	1035	135	2	1.03

Source: self-conducted survey and evaluation; see explanations in the text

(Lijphart, 1999; Tsebelis, 2002; Brouard & Hönnige, 2017; Stone, 1994). Ran Hirschl (2007, p. 73) even identified a "global trend toward juristocracy" which is "part of a broader process, whereby political and economic elites, while they profess support for democracy, attempt to insulate policymaking from the vicissitudes of democratic politics." This would mean that a small elite replaces elected members of parliament. "[I]n the end," Alec Stone Sweet similarly concludes, "governing with judges" is equal to "governing like judges" (Stone Sweet, 2000, p. 204). On the other hand, Hönnige (2011, p. 347) deplores the fact that we know "precious little about judicial systems outside the United States." That seems to hold true for pretty much everything that concerns constitutional adjudication, at least according to James L. Gibson et al. (1998), whom Hönnige calls as witnesses to his case. Gibson et al. (1998, p. 343) stated that we "understand little or nothing about the degree to which various judiciaries are politicized; how judges make decisions; how, whether, and to what extent those decisions are implemented; how ordinary citizens influence courts, if at all; or what effect courts have on institutions and cultures."

Based on this discrepancy between assumed importance of and missing knowledge about constitutional adjudication, Hönnige (2011, p. 355) calls for more "comparative research about constitutional courts." More than that, he says, this research should go "beyond judicialization" and include justices' preferences, macro-analytical perspectives, as well as inter- and intra-institutional rules. In short, Hönnige argues for combining U.S.-originating rational choice theories, or strategic accounts regarding the causes of judicial decision-making, with European approaches concerning the effects of constitutional adjudication on politics. In this last part, I will respond to Hönnige's call—at least partly and in a specific way. Distinct from Hönnige's approach, I want to shed some light on a blind spot in the research on constitutional adjudication, namely on those courts that this booklet is all about: the constitutional courts of the states. I hope to find out whether and how far German state constitutional courts contribute to what researchers have coined "judicialization" (Landfried, 1984; Hirschl, 2007: 169–210; Stone, 1994). As pointed out, the judicialization hypothesis "assumes that courts reduce the ability of government and parliament to take purely political decisions" (Hönnige, 2011, p. 347). At the same time, and as Hönnige (2011) suggested, I go "beyond the judicialization hypothesis" because I not only explore court rulings' possible effects on the legislature, but will also identify such rulings' possible causes. In short, I examine to which degree and for what reasons the constitutional courts of German states contribute to the judicialization of politics. In order to accomplish this task, I refer to neo-institutionalist approaches, which "seek to explain judicial decision-making as a process in which judicial values and attitudes are shaped by judges' distinct professional roles, their sense of obligation, and salient institutional perspectives" (Clayton, 1999, p. 32).

My approach differs in two respects from other studies on constitutional courts. First, as already pointed out, I focus on subnational constitutional courts. I therefore use the comparative method to study courts of last resort in a single country, that is, Germany. As Lijphart (1971, p. 683) has shown, the quality of any scientific explanation depends largely on how well it isolates the explanatory variables from those other variables that are presumably unrelated to the phenomenon under discussion. Limiting my analysis to cases in one country meets this requirement and allows me to test theories in the framework of a most-similar systems design. Second, most researchers of judicialization have based their studies on a relatively small number of rulings, then either supported or refuted the judicialization hypothesis depending on whether or not a court ruling nullifies a law. I will depart from this binary logic and try to capture the potential effects of rulings in a more nuanced and differentiated way, namely by determining the degree of judicialization by means of the "strength index" already discussed. This index measures the possible political reverberations of decisions made by state constitutional courts in Germany.

In common with many other researchers in comparative politics, I use an inference-oriented research design and quantitative methods in order to find causal links between independent and dependent variables (Geddes, 2003). The differences between the German states in size, population, and other aspects affect neither the status nor the competencies of the 16 state constitutional courts. The number of incoming cases is in no way linked to factors such as population or economic strength. All state constitutional courts are independent and autonomous institutions. Moreover, the states' highest courts comply with principles rooted in the civil law tradition. Hence, a most-similar systems research design and linear regression analysis seem appropriate tools to address my research question and to test and match theories, data, and applied methods (Geddes, 2003; Hirschl, 2005; Przeworski & Teune, 1970).

As laid out in Chap. 3, researchers have espoused various theories to strive to explain judicial behavior and decision-making (Rehder, 2007; Dyevre, 2010; Clayton, 1999). All have their merits. The challenge, then, is to find evidence that supports or rejects these approaches. A crucial step in such an endeavor is to develop hypotheses that can be tested empirically. Political scientists all agree that institutions such as norms, organizations, and rules matter (March & Olsen, 1989). This truism also applies to the ways in which scholars think about constitutional adjudication and constitutional courts. In 1988, Rogers M. Smith challenged the then dominant attitudinal approach by arguing that courts are institutions that influence how judges make their decisions. Similarly, Gillman and Clayton (1999, p. 3) pointed out that any attempt to explain "judicial behavior with reference to beliefs but not to contexts such as institutional settings will inevitably be incomplete." Arguably, this conception does not rule out justices having strategic goals that might play a role in judicial decision-making, but it gives preference to institutional factors in order to explain their decision-making. Institutions are thus not just a means for justices to realize some particular strategic goal, as Epstein and Knight assume (Knight, 1998, p. 12; Epstein & Knight, 2013). Instead, institutions represent ideas, provide structure, and prescribe roles for justices. The crucial question, then, is how to define and operationalize these dimensions. I focus on "different types of structures" that "constitute and empower political actors and their environments in important ways, endowing actors with specifiable constraints or capabilities or both" (Smith, 1988, p. 90). I try to capture these constraints and/or capabilities in

to make stronger decisions—either because they feel loyalty to the party that has picked and nominated them, or because they endorse other political values than those professed by the incumbent government. These justices may be inclined to limit the executive's room for maneuver and thus make strong decisions (H8 in model 2).

In sum, I will test seven hypotheses of which five, if corroborated, would underscore institutional theories (H1, H2, H3, H4, H5) while two, if confirmed, would indicate that justices' own strategic goals at least partially explain their court's decisions (H6, H7, H8).

Case selection and data collection are as crucial for empirical research as theories and hypotheses (Geddes, 2003, pp. 131–174; Epstein & Winter, 2014, pp. 63–94), and this naturally applies to the present study as well. In consequence, I will describe first (a) the process of case selection, then how I operationalized the (b) independent and (c) dependent variables. Table 7.4 outlines the independent variables used in the two regression analyses.

(a) *Case selection*: The following criteria underpinned which cases I selected for my two analyses, and consequently defined the number of decisions I included. First, I included all 16 state constitutional courts. However, as laid out in Chaps. 1 and 4, four states established their constitutional courts prior to the passing of the Basic Law in 1949, five in the 1950s, and the five formerly East German states, Berlin, and Schleswig-Holstein after unification (Table 1.1). As pointed out, state constitutional courts are not only supposed to be a defining feature of German federalism but also reflect historical circumstances. However, the fall

Table 7.4 Independent Variables: Descriptive Statistics

	N	Mean	Standard deviation	Minimum	Maximum
Model 1					
• (v1) Type of ruling	1116	0.5	0.5	0.0	1
• (v2) Type of proceeding	1116	0.3	0.5	0.0	1
• (v3) Jurisdiction	1116	7.7	5.9	0.1	15.0
• (v4) Possible terms	1116	52.4	43.5	0.0	100.0
• (v5) Age of court	1116	26.8	24.1	0.3	72.4
• (v6) Professional justices	1116	57.3	23.4	0.0	100.0
• (v7) Lay justices	1116	9.1	12.2	0.0	42.9
Model 2					
• (v1) Type of ruling	735	0.3	0.5	0.0	1
• (v2) Type of proceeding	735	0.3	0.5	0.0	1
• (v3) Jurisdiction	735	10.0	5.3	0.1	14.9
• (v4) Possible terms	735	49.1	47.6	0.0	100.0
• (v5) Age of court	735	26.1	25.4	0.3	72.4
• (v6) Professional justices	735	58.1	27.6	0.0	100.0
• (v7) Lay justices	735	7.6	11.5	0.0	33.3
• (v8) Oppositional justices	735	26.7	17.6	0.0	71.4

Source: Self-compiled

of the Wall and subsequent German unification gave rise to a kind of "constitutional fervour" (Delledonne, 2012, p. 303) that sparked new constitutions and inspired lawmakers to update the old ones with amendments encompassing new fundamental rights and policy goals (Reutter & Lorenz, 2016). This also affected the way constitution-makers conceived the role of constitutional courts. Moreover, I needed information on the justices' main professions and political attitudes. Professional data can be found in parliamentary records, the *Handbuch der Justiz* (Deutscher Richterbund, 1993ff.), court websites, and other sources. Information on political attitudes, however, is more difficult to glean. As there exist no records on how judges vote on crucial issues, I assume that the parliamentary parties nominate justices who overlap with their own political leanings. However, only a few regional parliaments report which parliamentary groups nominate the judiciary candidates for the constitutional court. This lack of information forced me to split my analysis accordingly: While Model 1 includes the decisions of all state constitutional courts, Model 2 only refers to those eight courts that provided data on the nominating parliamentary parties. Second, and as previously pointed out, I apply the aforementioned strength index. Pócza and Dobos (2019, p. 25f.), who were part of this research effort, recommend an exclusive focus on politically "salient decisions." Yet this is a difficult approach to take, and one open to subjective interpretation. I hence selected a different approach, including only those decisions that the state constitutional courts themselves found important enough to be featured in an official series published each year, produced by several such courts (LVerfGE, 1993ff.). This ultimately left me with 1116 decisions made by all constitutional courts, and with 735 decisions made by courts of which I was able to retrieve data about which parliamentary parties nominated the justices.

(b) *Independent variables*: I captured the institutional dimensions with five variables:

- Type of ruling (v1): As sub-national constitutional courts make only two types of decisions I created a categorical variable (dummy). I assume that a judgment ("2") will cause stronger decisions than a resolution ("1"). The decisions provide the information for the coding.
- Age of court (v2): This continuous variable measures the period between the election of a constitutional courts' first justices and the date a court hands down its decision. The data can be found in parliamentary records and in the decisions handed down by the courts.
- Jurisdiction (v3): Lijphart (1999, p. 225) has pointed out that it is not only the formal existence of the court's competencies that matters but also "the frequency of its use by the courts." I followed Lijphart's two-dimensional concept. To calculate the continuous variable, I combined two factors, namely the number of formal competencies and the number of incoming cases per year. This reads as follows: jurisdiction = number of legal competencies × number of incoming cases per year/100. The number of legal

Table 7.6 Strength of decisions and judicialization—Model 2 (Linear Regression and Bootstrapping)

	Linear Regression				Bootstrapping			
	CoefB	t	StandCoef (Beta)	VIF	Distortion	Bootstrap Error	Normal-based (95% CI)	
(const)	0.114	0.382			−0.002	0.299	−0.477	0.707
(v1) Type of ruling	0.585***	4.009	0.155	1.238	−0.002	0.154	0.282	0.891
(v2) Type of proceeding	1.112***	6.806	0.280	1.395	0.003	0.210	0.710	1.531
(v3) Jurisdiction	0.005	0.280	0.015	2.315	0.000	0.018	−0.030	0.040
(v4) Possible terms	0.001	0.521	0.030	2.744	−1.47E-5	0.002	−0.003	0.005
(v5) Age of court	0.002	0.359	0.021	2.922	0.000	0.005	−0.009	0.012
(v6) Professional justices	−0.004	−1.411	−0.072	2.154	−9.00E-5	0.003	−0.011	0.001
(v7) Lay justices	0.004	0.553	0.026	1.831	0.000	0.009	−0.013	0.022
(v8) oppositional justices	0.003	0.751	0.031	1.424	7.81E-5	0.004	−0.005	0.012
Obs.	735							
F	12.439***							
R^2	0.121							
Adjusted R^2	0.111							

*** = $p < 0.001$; ** = $p < 0.05$; * = $p < 0.10$
I used SPSS for the analysis; *p*

(adj. $r^2 = 0.142/0.111$). According to Cohen (1992), both values represent a medium-sized effect, Model 2's value is slightly lower. In both models, the variables 3–7 have no significant measurable influence on the strength of constitutional court decisions. Although competence profile (V3), the share of professional justices and the possibility of re-election (V4) were significant at the 5% level in model 1, their influence on the dependent variable can be ignored since both correlation coefficients were around 0. The only variables that were highly significant and had a measurable influence in both models were v1 (type of ruling) and v2 (type of decision). In the first model, a high proportion of professional judges (v6) was also significant, but its influence on the dependent variable can be ignored because the correlation coefficient was close to 0.

Any regression model operates on assumptions that should be fulfilled. First, independent variables should not correlate too strongly (multi-collinearity). This condition is fulfilled, as the VIF values are all well below ten. Moreover, residuals should not show auto-correlation. Once again, this criterion is met, as the Durbin-Watson-Test produces a value of 1.812, which is close enough to the ideal point of

2. However, the residuals fail to be normally distributed and there is heteroscedacity. As two requirements for a regression analysis are not met, I used bootstrapping as a non-parametric regression. Bootstrapping does not assume a normal distribution of the residuals, allows a variance in homoscedacity, and is less sensitive to outliers. In bootstrapping, the original sample is used to create new samples of the same size (the number of replications in this study is 10,000). Eventually, this approach allows one to replace the theoretical distribution function with an empirically created one (Efron, 1979). As expected, bootstrapping increased the standard errors and decreased significance for some variables. Based on this output, I can draw the following conclusions.

Both the age of the court and the share of professional judges are not significant and have no impact on the strength of decisions. In consequence, I could not confirm the hypotheses H2 and H6. The other variables are all significant to at least the 5% level but explain dependent variable's variance to different degrees. The type of decision shows the strongest effect (adj $r^2 = 0.2009$) followed by the type of proceeding (adj $r^2 = 0.1027$) and the jurisdiction (adj. $r^2 = 0.0344$). The variable that captures the number of possible terms is significant but shows a negative coefficient, meaning that if a justice can be re-appointed he or she will tend to make weaker decisions. The behaviorist variable that is significant (at the 5% level) is the proportion of justices nominated by a party in opposition. However, this has no effect on the variance of the dependent variable, as it triggers only an adjusted r^2 of -0.0040. In sum, my analysis strongly underscores the influence of institutional factors in both models.

Based on these findings, I can draw four tentative conclusions that pertain to my research question about the causes and consequences of judicial decision-making in German sub-national constitutional courts. First, to rule *with* a constitutional court does not necessarily mean to rule *like* a constitutional court, as Alec Stone (1994; Stone Sweet, 2000) and others have claimed. At least as far as German state constitutional courts are concerned, few rulings qualify as strong enough to encroach upon the legislature's competencies. Most rulings had no effect whatsoever on the legislature or on the government. In consequence, there is no simple causal link between the existence of a high court and judicialization. Rather, my findings indicate that one must take not only the type of constitutional court but also the context in which it operates into account (Clayton, 1999).

Second, my analysis of 1116 resp. 735 decisions of German state constitutional courts supports neo-institutionalist approaches. I have failed to turn up any evidence in favor of the assumption that justices' political preferences or professional attitudes have had any impact on the strength of German sub-national constitutional courts' decisions. Moreover, I have discovered that two factors are most important to explaining the strength of decisions: namely, the type of decision and the type of proceeding.

Third, my study has raised some methodological questions as well. Notably, the operationalization of variables remains a major challenge. This includes not only the enduring debate around how to capture justices' political attitudes but also how to measure constitutional courts' jurisdictions, as Hönnige (2011) has pointed out.

in Bundesländern. Theoretische Perspektiven, methodische Überlegungen und empirische Befunde (pp. 77–98). Springer VS.
Leunig, S. (2023). *Die Regierungssysteme der deutschen Länder im Vergleich* (3rd ed.). Springer VS.
Lijphart, A. (1971). Comparative politics and the comparative method. *American Political Science Review, 65*(3), 682–693.
Lijphart, A. (1999). *Patterns of democracy: Government forms and performance in thirty-six countries*. Yale University Press.
Lorenz, A. (2017). Das Verfassungsgericht des Landes Brandenburg als politisiertes Organ. In W. Reutter (Ed.), *Landesverfassungsgerichte: Entwicklung—Aufbau—Funktionen* (pp. 105–128). Springer VS.
LVerfGE. (1993). *Entscheidungen der Verfassungsgerichte der Länder.* Ed. by Members of the Courts. Vols. 1–26, Walter de Gruyter.
March, J. G., & Olsen, J. P. (1989). *Rediscovering institutions: The organizational basis of politics*. Free Press.
Meyer, P., & Hönnige, C. (2017). Der Niedersächsische Staatsgerichtshof. In W. Reutter (Ed.), *Landesverfassungsgerichte. Entwicklung–Aufbau–Funktionen* (pp. 219–242). Springer VS.
Pócza, K., & Dobos, G. (2019). Research methodology. In K. Pócza (Ed.), *Constitutional politics and the judiciary: Decision-making in Central and Eastern Europe* (pp. 8–31). Routledge.
Pócza, K., Dobos, G., & Gyulai, A. (2017). How to measure the strength of judicial decisions: A methodological framework. *German Law Journal, 18*(6), 1557–1586. Retrieved from https://papers.ssrn.com/sol3/papers.cfm?abstract_id=3082168
Pritchett, C. H. (1948). *The Roosevelt Court: A study in judicial politics and values 1937-1947.* Quid Pro Books.
Przeworski, A., & Teune, H. (1970). *The logic of comparative social inquiry*. Krieger Publishing.
Rehder, B. (2007). *What is political about jurisprudence: Courts, politics and political science in Europe and the United States*. Discussion Paper 07/5, MPIfG.
Reutter, W. (2020a). Verfassungsgerichtsbarkeit in Bundesländern und Justizialisierung – zur Einführung. In W. Reutter (Ed.), *Verfassungsgerichtsbarkeit in Bundesländern. Theoretische Perspektiven, methodische Überlegungen und empirische Befunde* (pp. 1–22). Springer VS.
Reutter, W. (2020b). Zum Status der Landesverfassungsgerichte als Verfassungsorgane. In W. Reutter (Ed.), *Verfassungsgerichtsbarkeit in Bundesländern: Theoretische Perspektiven, methodische Überlegungen und empirische Befunde* (pp. 155–174). Springer VS.
Reutter, W., & Lorenz, A. (2016). Explaining the Frequency of Constitutional Change in the German Länder: Institutional and Party Factors. *Publius: The Journal of Federalism, 46*(1), 103–127.
Rinken, A. (1994). Die Rechtsprechung des Staatsgerichtshofs der Freien Hansestadt Bremen. *Jahrbuch des öffentlichen Rechts der Gegenwart, 42*, 325–399.
Rinken, A. (2000). Landesverfassungsgerichtsbarkeit im Bundesstaat. *NordÖR – Zeitschrift für öffentliches Recht in Norddeutschland, 3*(3), 89–96.
Segal, J. A., & Spaeth, H. J. (2002). *The Supreme Court and the attitudinal model revisited.* Cambridge University Press.
Smith, R. M. (1988). Political jurisprudence, the "new institutionalism," and the future of public law. *American Political Science Review, 82*(1), 89–108.
Steinsdorff, S. v. (2010). Verfassungsgerichte als Demokratie-Versicherung? Ursachen und Grenzen der wachsenden Bedeutung juristischer Politikkontrolle. In K. H. Schrenk & M. Soldner (Eds.), *Analyse demokratischer Regierungssysteme* (pp. 479–498). Springer VS.
Stone, A. (1994). Judging socialist reform: The politics of coordinate construction in France and Germany. *Comparative Political Studies, 26*(4), 443–469.
Stone Sweet, A. (2000). *Governing with Judges. Constitutional politics in Europe*. Oxford University Press.
Tsebelis, G. (2002). *Veto players: How political institutions work*. University Press.
Voßkuhle, A. (2011). Die Landesverfassungsgerichtsbarkeit im föderalen und europäischen Verfassungsgerichtsverbund. *Jahrbuch des öffentlichen Rechts der Gegenwart, 59*, 215–243.

Chapter 8
State Constitutional Courts and "Militant Democracy"

As highlighted in Chap. 4, German constitutional courts can be understood as an "institutional response" to authoritarian or totalitarian regimes: If need be, they should have the means to defend constitutional democracy. Should other political institutions fail to make democracy resilient against populism or authoritarianism, constitutional courts must act as safeguards to keep democratic rule in place. They may even solve Karl Popper's "paradox of democracy," i.e., that a democratic majority might decide to abolish democracy and install a non-democratic tyrant (Popper, 1962, p. 265 [Fn 4], cf. also Rijpkema, 1993). In such a scenario, a non-majoritarian institution like a constitutional court could serve as an effective check on the enemies of democracies and make it impossible "to exploit the freedoms inherent in democracy" (Kommers & Miller, 2012, p. 285). In addition, constitutional courts should have the necessary jurisdictions not only to uphold democracy, but also to force authoritarian governments to comply with the constitution. So far, the discussion in Germany has focused on the Federal Constitutional Court and its jurisdictions with regard to what Germany has coined "*wehrhafte Demokratie*," or "militant democracy." Most importantly, the Federal Constitutional Court is entitled to ban parties, prevent government from unconstitutionally abusing its power, or rule that an individual "has forfeited his or her individual rights" (Kommers & Miller, 2012, p. 285). That, at least, was the theory for a very long time. However, the recent examples of Poland and Hungary have proven how easy it is not only to neutralize constitutional courts, but even to use them for authoritarian or populist purposes. Now, alongside these Polish and Hungarian developments, the rise of the extremist AfD—its strength seemingly growing with every election—has sparked debates about how to shore up the resilience of Germany's constitution. One proposal is to immunize the Federal Constitutional Court against populist attacks.

Recently, state constitutional courts have entered the fray. With several state elections looming in 2024, the possibility of the AfD becoming the strongest party of a state raises questions about how state constitutional courts may be affected and whether they can prevent, or at least contain, possible AfD-led governments. In this

W. Reutter, *Constitutional Courts in the German States*, Contributions to Political Science, https://doi.org/10.1007/978-3-031-64751-2_8

8.2 Making State Constitutional Courts Resilient

A ghost is haunting Thuringia—and some other German states—and that ghost's name is the potential inability of the constitutional court to make decisions. The conditions for such a scenario are well known. The AfD needs just over one third of the seats in the respective state parliament to torpedo the election of members to the "supreme guardian of the state constitution" and thus render the respective state constitutional court incapable of making decisions. "But where there is danger,/ there also grows rescue," as Friedrich Hölderlin already knew, and in this case rescue means: "self-supplementation" (*Selbstergänzung*). For with such a "fallback provision" a state constitutional court would be able to fill vacant judicial posts independently of the parties and the parliament and thus banish the specter of incapacity. The state constitutional courts could protect themselves and thus, ultimately, democracy within their borders.

The possibility of vacancies leading to an inability to make decisions is not limited to the Constitutional Court of Thuringia, although the reasons for the particular prominence of its case are well known: In the upcoming state elections of September 2024, the AfD could win more than a third of the seats in Thuringia's state parliament. It is uncertain how said parliament would then be able to elect successors for retiring members of the constitutional court with the required two-thirds majority. Moreover, the Thuringian parliament has already failed several times to prevent vacancies on its constitutional court—even the position of the court's president was temporarily vacant three times.

In President Manfred Aschke's case, this electoral delay was not significant. Aschke became President on May 22nd, 2014, succeeding Joachim Lindner, whose term ended on April 30th, 2014, as he had reached the age of 68 and was no longer eligible. Consequently, the presidential position remained unoccupied for about 3 weeks. When Manfred Aschke himself reached the age limit and had to leave office in March 2018, it took the Thuringian parliament 3 months to install his successor. This successor, Stefan Kaufmann, was not elected, sworn in, and appointed until June 21st, 2018. In spite of this poor record, Thuringia's parliament showed no improvement going forward. On the contrary: The presidential office's handover to Klaus von der Weiden was postponed until June 21st, 2022, even though Kaufmann had resigned on December 29th, 2021. None of these presidents left office due to unexpected circumstances such as death or resignation. Rather, they lost their eligibility to serve on the court upon reaching the age of 68, as stated in § 4 Abs. 1 ThürVerfGHG. The Thuringian Constitutional Court Law initially provided no guidelines for handling presidential vacancies or incapacity. As a result, the court's longest-serving professional justice performed the presidential duties in the interim (Weiden, 2019, p. 211). It was only in 2022 that the position of Vice-President was eventually established through a simple law.

The Thuringian parliament is not the only state parliament that fails to elect constitutional court justices in a timely manner. For instance, justices retiring from the Berlin Constitutional Court sit in an "acting" capacity for an average of 5 months because the Berlin House of Representatives (*Abgeordnetenhaus*) has repeatedly failed to elect successors for justices leaving office. Consequently, many justices have been forced to continue their duties until their successor's election. Interestingly, out of the nine justices tasked with ruling on the constitutionality of the 2021 election to the Berlin House of Representatives, six were acting justices whose terms had already expired. Furthermore, the newly elected House of Representatives in 2022 fared no better than the previous one, as it failed to elect new justices until the spring of 2024. Temporary vacancies lasting from 2 to 20 months can even be found at the Federal Constitutional Court (Weiden, 2019, p. 213). However, none of these vacancies fundamentally jeopardized the functioning of the respective court, regardless of their duration. Yet the cases raise the question of how to ensure the functioning of a constitutional court when the parliament fails to fulfill its electoral duties or does so belatedly.

Klaus von der Weiden, the current President of the Thuringian Constitutional Court, argues that legal precautions can never render a constitutional court inoperative. He asserts that there exist both a guarantee to justice (*Justizgewährleistungsgarantie*) and a right to a statutory judge (*Recht auf den gesetzlichen Richter*) that preclude the possibility of a non-functioning constitutional court (Weiden, 2019, p. 212). He believes that a constitutional court *must* function, and that there are legal or constitutional provisions that support this claim under all circumstances. Klaus von der Weiden identifies three options that allow constitutional courts to operate no matter what: the continuation principle (*Amtsfortführungsprinzip*), the principle of deputies (*Stellvertreterprinzip*), and the bench reduction principle (*Richterreduzierungsprinzip*) (Weiden, 2019, p. 213). These options can be found in different combinations in the states. Table 8.1 presents some examples. Berlin and Brandenburg apply the bench reduction principle along with the continuation principle. The Berlin Constitutional Court and the Brandenburg State Constitutional Court generally require six constitutional justices to be present to form a quorum empowered to hand down a decision. Yet this quorum can be further reduced if partiality concerns require the exclusion of certain constitutional justices from the case, or if no successors have as yet been appointed for retired justices (§ 11 (1) Berl-VerfGHG).

Thuringia, meanwhile, utilizes the principles of both continuity of office and deputization (Lembcke, 2017, pp. 939–396; Reutter, 2019). Members and deputies remain in office after the end of their statutory term until a successor is elected (§ 3 (2) ThürVerfGHG). § 8 (1) ThürVerfGHG contains detailed provisions for the replacement of a member or deputy in the event of his or her incapacity or impediment. These provisions also apply in the event of a vacancy, i.e., if a successor is not elected in time and a seat on the constitutional court remains unoccupied. According to Klaus von der Weiden, the Thuringian Constitutional Court is adequately staffed. This is thanks to the possibility of substitution, even in the case of retirement due to age—a crucial protection to prevent the parliament from deliberately rendering the constitutional court incapable of functioning. This can happen in various situations, such as when the radical forces form a blocking minority of one-third of parliament, or when a parliamentary majority seeks to evade the court's control. According to in the eighth legislative term: two deputies (to be elected in 2025) and one member (to be elected in 2026). Since the sitting parliament elected one member on February 4th, 2022, the president on May 5th, 2022, and six other members and three deputies on September 23rd, 2022, the eighth parliament would have to fill almost the entire constitutional court at the end of the legislative period. To make matters worse, in the case of a 7-year term, the successor would have to be elected in February, May, and September 2029, i.e., during the (pre)election campaign phase for the ninth parliament. It seems unlikely that an already polarized parliament could succeed in almost completely filling its constitutional court under such conditions. This would be all the more dramatic because the constitutional court itself is the ideal instrument to calm political conflicts and decide disputes between organs. But how could the co-option of justices through the court itself help in such a situation?

In order to answer this question and discuss the practicality of the proposed fallback mechanism of co-optation, I distinguish between two scenarios, both of which could occur in the eighth legislative term. The first scenario looks like this: If the eighth state parliament, elected on September 1st, 2024, does not succeed in appointing the two retiring deputies in 2025 and one new member in 2026, co-optation would be a perfectly viable option. The state's constitutional court, as a fallback electoral body, would have enough time and a sufficient number of members/deputies still elected by the state parliament to co-opt new members/deputies. Under these conditions, the court could easily maintain its decision-making and functional capacity. Co-optation would have prevented, or at least made less likely, a possible inability to take decisions.

The second case, occuring in 2029, would differ in several respects. If one considers the 6-month period proposed by Gundling, after which the constitutional court could self-appoint members the fallback electoral body could fill vacant seats at the court (including the president) in Fall 2029 or Spring 2030. For a period of 6 months, the court would be limited to making decisions only with members who are either currently in office or who it appointed itself. During this 6-month period—while the newly elected state parliament is constituted and, if necessary, a new prime minister is elected—the court would only be able to function based on the principle of continuation in office. In legal terms, this situation may not be problematic as long as no member or deputy resigns from office, becomes a member of the state government, is elected to parliament, or reaches the age of 68. The same applies to the fallback electoral body. In March 2030, Thuringia's constitutional court would consist of 16 members, only four of whom would have been elected by the state parliament as provided by law. This is contingent on the state parliament successfully electing successors for the retiring deputies in 2024. How exactly would this composition impact the constitutional court's position and decision-making ability? That remains unclear.

These two hypothetical scenarios illustrate the advantages and disadvantages of co-optation or self-appointment, which in Thuringia would only be feasible in combination with the principles of continuity of office and deputization. Under favorable conditions, if only one member/deputy needs to be co-opted, the fallback electoral body would still consist of a majority of members/deputies who have primary legitimacy mediated by the state parliament. There would be no risk of conflict between state bodies, making this variant appear practicable and effective. The fallback rule of self-supplementation could at least temporarily banish the specter of a constitutional court's inability to pass resolutions. This is no small feat.

However, under unfavorable conditions—i.e., if several members or deputies are to be elected and there is no parliamentary majority in sight—the fallback electoral body would consist predominantly of members or deputies who lack the "proper" legitimacy provided for by law. Under such circumstances, the co-optation of new members could very well create new problems. Crucially, such a constellation could occur at the end of the eighth parliamentary term. Should Thuringia's state parliament fail to elect members or deputies, its constitutional court will consist solely of co-opted or "acting" justices. Only four deputies would still be able to invoke a parliamentary mandate. According to Klaus von der Weiden, this may remain legally unobjectionable. Equally, however, it could easily prepare the ground for parties to refuse to obey the constitutional court and to discredit it as a constitutional body.

There remains another point to consider. Self-supplementation or co-optation cannot be achieved without democratic and constitutional costs. The election of constitutional justices by parliament not only ensures democratic legitimacy, but also underpins the principle of the separation of powers. Once in office, constitutional justices are not subject to any democratic control (apart from the possibility of removal from office). They are, and must be, rightly independent. However, self-recruitment would eliminate precisely the democratic control parliamentary selection and election provide. At the same time, a crucial question arises: Should members who have come into office through co-optation always be liable to replacement by members elected by parliament? Gundling suggested this caveat in order to curtail parliamentary rights as little as possible, yet it is one that would create judges who are "on call": Co-opted members or deputies could be recalled and replaced at any time.

Whether and to what extent a self-amendment can banish the specter of a constitutional court's incapacity to pass resolutions will therefore vary by circumstances. It all depends, as it were.

References

Beck, H., Jaschinski, J., Kordt, K., Müller-Elmau, M., & Talg, J. (2024). *Rechtsstaatliche Resilienz in Thüringen stärken. Handlungsempfehlungen aus der Szenarioanalyse des Thüringen-Projekts*. VerfBlog. https://doi.org/10.17176/20240416-103633-0

Glathe, J., & Varga, M. (2023). Defending democracy in the light of growing radicalization: Tensions within Germany's militant democracy. *DPCE Online, 59*(2), 2039–2054. Retrieved from https://www.dpceonline.it/index.php/dpceonline/article/view/1957

Gundling, L.C. (2024). *Selbstergänzung zur Vermeidung politischer Blockaden des Thüringer Verfassungsgerichtshofs, VerfBlog,* 2024/2/01. https://doi.org/10.59704/0649f858cd14f186

SPRINGER NATURE

GPSR Compliance

The European Union's (EU) General Product Safety Regulation (GPSR) is a set of rules that requires consumer products to be safe and our obligations to ensure this.

If you have any concerns about our products, you can contact us on ProductSafety@springernature.com

In case Publisher is established outside the EU, the EU authorized representative is:

Springer Nature Customer Service Center GmbH
Europaplatz 3
69115 Heidelberg, Germany